Deep Change

Professional Development from the Inside Out

Angela B. Peery

ScarecrowEducation
Lanham, Maryland • Toronto • Oxford
2004

Published in the United States of America
by ScarecrowEducation
An imprint of The Rowman & Littlefield Publishing Group, Inc.
4501 Forbes Boulevard, Suite 200, Lanham, Maryland 20706
www.scarecroweducation.com

PO Box 317
Oxford
OX2 9RU, UK

British Library Cataloguing in Publication Information Available

Library of Congress Cataloging-in-Publication Data

Peery, Angela B., 1964–
    Deep change : professional development from the inside out /
Angela B. Peery.
        p.   cm.
    Includes bibliographical references and index.
    ISBN 1–57886–048–2 (pbk. : alk. paper)
    1. Teachers—In-service training. 2. Continuing education. I. Title.
LB1731 .P365 2004
370'.71'5—dc22   2003018613

©™ The paper used in this publication meets the minimum
requirements of American National Standard for Information
Sciences—Permanence of Paper for Printed Library Materials,
ANSI/NISO Z39.48–1992. Manufactured in the United States of
America.

Contents

Acknowledgments

To the teachers whose words fill these pages, I offer sincere and humble gratitude. You do the work of the world every day, and I am privileged to be able to witness it, nurture it, and write about it. I truly stand in awe of the teaching that you do and of the learning you have brought forth in me.

To the readers who read and listened to the earlier versions of this book, my heartfelt thank you. You know who you are, and I am indebted.

Many other people have encouraged, supported, and inspired me over the years, but three special men deserve recognition upon the completion of this book.

The first is my father, Daniel Bushnell, one of my first teachers. Even though he literally had to lock me out of the house on sunny childhood afternoons so that I would stop reading and writing for a while and enjoy some physical play, he has always nurtured my love of study. As I grew up and became a teacher—and now, as I have ventured down new paths in education—he has never failed to remind me how much joy teaching brings my soul. Thank you, Dad, for forcing me to remember where my heart is: in the classroom, alongside teachers and students.

The second is the best mentor one could ever ask for, Paul Browning. He was the only administrator in Horry County Schools who would take a chance on me when he hired me as an assistant principal (after seven unsuccessful applications). He allowed me to pursue my loves (curriculum, instruction, and professional development) while challenging me to work in less familiar areas (student supervision, athletics, finance, and personnel). The four years I spent with him at Socastee High School were the best training I could receive in the public education system. Paul is also the person who inspired me to write this book, beginning with a presentation I made at the NASSP Annual Convention in March 2002. He goaded me into proposing a session, and one door after another has since opened. I am continuously motivated by his optimism, humor, and genuine love of his work. I'm thankful every day for the opportunities he gave me and for his thoughtful comments on my own writing, teaching, and professional and personal growth.

The third is my best friend and husband, Timothy Peery. During the year I wrote my dissertation, he kept our household running smoothly. As I complete this book, he has once again paid our bills, cared for our pets and home, and so on. Without Tim's assistance, I could not dedicate myself as I do to the two passions of my vocation: teaching and writing. Also, without his love, I would not have the faith in myself to attempt and complete all the tasks I undertake. Tim has loved me unconditionally in both good times and bad, and that's the most precious gift of my life. Putting my love and appreciation into words is simply impossible, so I will simply say "thank you, Tim" once again.

I've been an educator for seventeen challenging yet joyous years, spending most of that time teaching in high schools. I've been married to my dear husband, Tim, for about the same length of time. What I've learned from these coincidentally parallel experiences is that both teaching and marriage require a great deal of patience, nurturing, and optimism, and a strong sense of humor.

This book is about patience. It's about the patience we must all have as we strive to make big, important changes in our nation's schools. It's also about nurturing. The public, including our lawmakers, must nurture educators. And educators at all levels must nurture each other. My book is optimistic. I've been called an idealist at times, and I've been labeled a cynic once or twice, too. I like to think, however, that I'm a realistic optimist. In other words, if the glass is half full, let's say it's half full and then work to fill it higher. Lastly, this book is about having a sense of humor, a sense of lightness and joy, and a spirit of fun about our work and our lives. We must all remember to laugh at ourselves, laugh with our colleagues, and teach our students to laugh. It's healthy.

Now, a bit about the person behind this book. I'm a native Virginian who adopted the South Carolina coast as my home in 1989, and has never once missed the cold winters of the Shenandoah Valley or the snow of the Alleghany Mountains (although I do think it's nice to escape the extreme July humidity of the coast and head north to visit). I do not have biological children but am an incredible animal lover who currently "mothers" two Labrador retrievers and a cat. I'm the product of a blue-collar, working-class, divorced family of the disco-age 1970s. No one in my immediate family ever went to college, but I knew education was my ticket to a better life, so I bested them all. I persevered and ended up with a doctorate. I would go to school forever if I could; I suppose that's why I've chosen to stay in education all these years.

The most important thing to know before reading this book is that I'm passionate about working with teachers, students, family members, and friends to continuously learn new things. I've been a secondary English teacher, part-time undergraduate and graduate school instructor, educational consultant, and writer. I currently serve the state of South Carolina as a "teacher specialist on site" and was a high school assistant principal for four years prior to that. Some of the hats I've worn include school-level and district-level curriculum coach, department chairperson, consultant, test designer, researcher . . . and the list goes on and on. Staying busy is enjoyable for me, and I have often been in at least two of the previously mentioned roles at one time.

Helping make education better for all participants in the system has been a cornerstone of my life. I hope that through this book you find some way to make education better for someone (yourself, a colleague, students) wherever it is you may be. As Craig Kridel, an awe-inspiring professor and member of my doctoral committee used to say, "Cheers!" Onward and upward we go.

CHAPTER 1

Why Staff Development Must Change

"Change is the nursery of music, joy, life and eternity."

—John Donne in "Elegy III, Change"

"They must often change, who would be constant in happiness or wisdom."

—Confucius

"A change will do you good," sings musician Sheryl Crow in one of her biggest hits. Nearly everyone accepts that change is the single constant in our personal and professional lives. As an educator, I believe most changes in public education are undertaken in order to "do good." Make no mistake: I do not advocate change merely for the sake of change. Nor do I subscribe to the widespread adage, "If it ain't broke, don't fix it." There is middle ground between both of those extremes. There is the power of possibility. If something can be improved, by all means, people should pull together to create change. Where better to effect positive change than in public education, which is increasingly targeted by legislators, media, and citizens as something that must be improved?

The best way to improve education for our nation's youth is simpler than most people think. We must improve the ongoing education of the adults who facilitate student learning. Professional development for teachers must change significantly.

Years of personal research and direct experience have led me to this firm conviction about the continuous learning of teachers. Many prominent educators—some of whom are widely published—have called for a virtual overhaul of professional development, but with little impact on the daily lives of the teaching workforce. Why should I add my input, and why should you give credence to my statements? Refer to the preface for some background on what kinds of research and experience I bring to the table. Also allow me to share with you some powerful thinking and concurring opinions from people whose names you probably know and whose work in education is internationally respected. I will spare you long explanations and detailed analyses of data but will summarize the most significant lessons I've put into practice from these noted experts who have served as distant mentors to me. While I admire and have learned from their work, the missing piece seems to be what I hope to add to the conversation: *ample evidence of transformed teaching, from diverse contexts.*

Before discussing the ideas of individuals, I'll cite the recommendations of the National Staff Development Council (NSDC). The NSDC bills itself as "the largest non-profit professional association committed to ensuring success for all students through staff development and school improvement" (http://www/nsdc/org/). Published in 2001, the NSDC's main recommendations center on the idea that effective staff development is that which results in increased learning for students. As such, effective staff development organizes adults into learning communities, requires skillful leadership, and uses resources to support adult learning and collaboration. It uses disaggregated student data to help adults in the system set priorities, monitor progress, and sustain continuous improvement. It uses multiple sources of information, helps educators apply research, incorporates knowledge about human learning and change, makes use of appropriate learning strategies, and provides educators with assistance in collaborating. Effective staff development helps educators appreciate diversity, create orderly learning environments, hold high expectations, and involve families and communities while deepening their own professional knowledge base (http://www.nsdc.org/library/standards2001html [accessed 30 September 2003]).

These recommendations may seem a tall order; however, they represent a synthesis of decades of research and practice in metacognition, adult learning, effective teaching, professional development, and education reform. They are ambitious yet appropriate for this period in history, as we try to educate more of our populace than ever before, and better than we ever have. Additionally, it is possible to honor the NSDC recommendations *with every group of educators, in every inservice offered, in every graduate course taught, and in every faculty meeting held.* The recommendations focusing on creating learning communities, providing collaboration, and understanding human learning will frame much of this book's discussion.

Adult learning theory (andragogy) is pertinent to any discussion of professional development for teachers or of continuing education in any occupation. Malcolm Knowles is the preeminent name in this field and is sometimes called the father of andragogy. The philosophical underpinnings of andragogy as related to learning new things are as follows: Adults need to know a reason for learning something; they need to learn experientially; they must approach learning as problem solving; and they learn best when the topic is of immediate relevance, meaning it can be applied right away in their personal and/or professional lives (Knowles 1984).

For teachers in professional development situations, the theory of andragogy implies that the growth process is much more important than transmission of any specific content. This is a crucial point: the "how" should always take precedence over the "what." In other words, the journey is more important than the destination. The "how" (the methods used in the process of learning) is what teachers will internalize and use to approach future new content. Inservice facilitators, graduate school instructors, and staff development leaders should, then, seek to employ methods like reflection, self-evaluation, personalized inquiry, simulations, dialogue, coaching, and direct application of new strategies. They must act as collaborators and resources, more as colearners than supervisors or authorities. To summarize, from an andragogical perspective, good professional development should be the best form of problem-based learning.

Michael Fullan of the University of Toronto has done extensive research in education reform. In his 1989 book *The New Meaning of Educational Change*, he discusses the concept of "teacher as learner" at length. He advocates that administrators and systems support the ongoing learning of teachers by providing time, training, support, and resources. He promotes staff development that combines technical skills, reflective practice, inquiry, and collaboration. He believes these components result in true lifelong learning.

Fullan believes that teachers must lead education reform and that they are the key to continuous improvement in schools. He has said, "Education reform will never amount to anything until teachers become . . . seamlessly inquiry-oriented, reflective, and collaborative professionals" (1991, 326). Helping teachers hone their questioning skills, reflect upon their work, and collaborate with their peers are hallmarks of effective professional development.

Parker Palmer is another name you may recognize. There are several core concepts in his work that I want to touch upon, as they are central to the discussion in this book. His idea of teaching "who we are" goes hand in hand with the principles of andragogy. It focuses upon the intellectual, emotional, and spiritual lives of teachers, and most interestingly, the union of all three. As Palmer notes, "The ultimate source of good teaching lies not in technique but in the identity of the teacher, in those persistent but obscure forces that constitute one's nature" (http://www.teacherformation.org/html/rr/intro-f.cfm [accessed 30 September 2003]). Therefore, if one agrees with Palmer, helping teachers better know themselves helps improve not only their teaching but also the overall quality of their lives both inside and outside school.

Palmer's notion of "living divided" also has relevance to our discussion. By living divided, Palmer means a person's basic values are being undermined by his work or another situation in which he finds himself. An example of this is teacher and writer Ruby Hart, whom you will meet later. Ruby left teaching because she felt she was being forced to live divided; her spirit was constantly under attack in her school. Many teachers leave the profession for reasons related to the concept of living divided. Talk to teachers in the current climate of high-stakes testing and punitive accountability measures, and you will hear refrains of how they are feeling divided, as if the profession they entered with love and enthusiasm has become robotic, lifeless, and stressful for them. I call it "being schizophrenic." We must do what we are told, many times even though we know it's not best for us or for students, and put on a happy face while doing it. At the end of the day, we feel as if we have been two people and no longer know what is right and real.

Palmer advocates many interesting processes for reenergizing one's teaching, including having collegial dialogue, exploring poetry and other art forms, using a Quaker process called the "clearness committee," and engaging in periods of reflective silence as well as keeping journals. These ideas have merged to form the basics of the Courage to Teach (CTT), a fellowship program for educators. Because I was part of an initial CTT group and was profoundly changed, I have adapted some of the processes in my work with various groups of teachers. I have incorporated some of the strategies my CTT instructor used as I use professional dialogue in addition to personal and professional poetry, art, and journals. One repeatedly successful activity is the exploration of metaphors, especially as they apply to one's teaching. Palmer promotes thinking about such metaphors:

> [An] approach to good talk about good teaching is to explore metaphors and images about who we are, what we are doing and what we would like to be and do—when we teach. That is the value of metaphor: it offers us a way of glimpsing from the corner of the eye things that elude us when we try to view them directly. By articulating and exploring the metaphors that arise when we reflect on our own teaching, we touch the deep dimensions of self and vocation that defy headlong analysis (http://www.teacherformation.org/html/rr/intro-f.cfm [accessed 30 September 2003]).

Metaphors cannot be quantified; they cannot be scored or checked off on a list of desirable teaching behaviors. They are pliable and rich with layers of meaning. Perhaps that is why encouraging metaphorical thinking works so well in this era of ever-increasing statistical analysis, standardization, and legal accountability. Teachers want to visualize and analyze their work on many levels, and asking them to explore teaching metaphors allows for deep reflection in an otherwise "hard data" environment. (Examples of teachers writing, drawing, and discussing their personal teaching metaphors follows in chapter 4.)

Donald Schön's name is virtually synonymous with the word "reflection," and he is best known for his books *The Reflective Practitioner* (1983) and *Educating the Reflective Practitioner* (1987). The ideas that apply most directly to educators' professional development are his concepts of error as a source of discovery, reflection-in-action, and reflection-on-action.

Reflection-in-action is what we typically call "thinking on our feet."

It involves thinking about our past experiences, immediately assessing our emotions, and employing actions that we feel will be successful in any given situation. Then we build new understandings, perhaps to utilize in future situations of a similar nature. Schön calls this instant response an "experiment," and it is an essential component of all adult learning (1983, 68).

When reflection-in-action brings about positive results, we sometimes minimize this as luck, but it is actually the end product of a sophisticated process that our brains handle smoothly and swiftly. Many teachers dismiss this type of successful teaching practice simply as "learning as you go" and implicitly knowing what to do; in fact, it often has sophisticated theory embedded within it. These actions are truly examples of "not knowing what you know" in many cases, and the astute staff developer must help the teacher articulate theoretical stances from these actions. Then the teacher can better reconcile theory with practice and personalize it in order to determine future actions in a more well-informed manner. (This kind of "digging deep" into practice to find the roots of theory will be discussed in more detail in chapter 4.)

Conversely, when an experiment does not create the desired results, "try, try again" must prevail. Talking and brainstorming with colleagues is one way to find alternative actions to add to one's teaching repertoire. It is the job of the effective staff developer to orchestrate the kind of dialogue that helps teachers align theory and practice and support each other in creating new responses to problematic classroom situations. Continuously searching for new ideas is hard work and must be supported in ongoing staff development. Palmer notes that "it is difficult to trust the pool of possibilities is bottomless, that one can keep diving in and finding more" (2000, 107), but this kind of exploration should be a focal point of professional inservice education. Staff developers must nurture abundance-thinking and avoid having a "one right answer" or scarcity mentality.

Reflection-on-action is another essential component of adult learning, but differs from reflection-in-action because it occurs after a problem occurs. As educators, we engage in many forms of this type of reflection: we may talk with trusted colleagues or family members, quietly and privately think through the situation at length, or write and sketch in a teaching journal. By reflecting, we create questions about our past practice and conduct trial runs of techniques we want to use. In the average teacher's day or week, however, how much time is devoted to any sort of reflection-on-action? In my experience, not much. That is why reflection-on-action in the forms of presentations or publications of successful practice, honest and safe dialogue with colleagues, and writing in teaching journals is so important. These methods must be employed in faculty meetings, graduate courses, and all staff development offerings to some extent for maximum effectiveness and transfer. (Chapters 3 and 4 contain examples of various forms of reflection-on-action.)

For Schön, learning involves the discovery and correction of error. In education these days, it is difficult to see "error" as anything but negative, especially with increased pressures to improve learning outcomes. However, as educators, we should see every error as an opportunity to change for the better, and not as a "mistake." As Fullan has said, "Problems are our friends" (1993, 21). I once had a boss who used the word "probletunities," and I now proudly use this word myself. After all, don't we tell students that one learns a great deal from failure?

When a lesson goes wrong in the classroom, many teachers look for another strategy that will work within the current constraints. A solution within the established rules is set into motion; constraints are not necessarily questioned. According to Schön, another way to respond is to question the parameters within which one is operating. This inquiry may lead to a shift in the way in which strategies and possible results are framed. In other words, a teacher may discover new strategies if she can *perceive* and *alter* the framework. Taking this kind of questioning stance is essential when examining one's teaching. Sometimes it requires questioning seemingly set variables like time, grading, grouping patterns, and even the amount of noise emanating from one's room. If you are a classroom teacher, don't be lured into thinking that you don't have more control over some of these parameters than you think, even though administrators may try to convince you otherwise. Explore and question constraints that you haven't before, and you may find exciting new answers. (Examples of error as impetus for change and improved effectiveness are discussed in chapters 3 and 4.)

Ann Lieberman has done much work in the field of effective teaching. She is the author of *Teachers: Transforming Their World and Their Work*, in addition to many other titles. She is an emeritus professor from Teachers College at Columbia University, and is currently a senior scholar at the Carnegie Foundation for the Advancement of Teaching and a visiting professor at Stanford University. Lieberman has been studying staff development and working collaboratively with teachers for over thirty years. In one of her most recent speeches, she said "development should grow out of the kind of changes that people want to make initially, which usually means it can't be a predetermined package" (http://www.nsdc.org/library/jsd/lieberman204.html [accessed 30 September 2003]). Lieberman's words echo my emphasis on process over content. To illuminate this idea a bit further and provide a humorous slant on it, I quote my mentor and friend, Paul Browning: "Training is for dogs. *Development* is for people." Training in a specific program, set of materials, or faddish instructional strategy never suffices. Teachers must invest in their own growth by posing their own questions and studying topics of their own choice. *This personalization is the essence of development.* Administrators must be cautious when purchasing program materials or hiring trainers who have only one spiel. Without personal commitment from teachers, inservice inevitably fails. How can there be personal buy-in if a program or presentation is "one size fits all"?

Lieberman also understands that true learning often proceeds slowly. We are in a time of great urgency in education—administrators, legislators, and much of the tax-paying public want everything done yesterday, including increased test scores, higher graduation and college matriculation rates, improved behavior, reduced teen pregnancy, and a host of other desired end results. Lieberman (2002) has said:

> While pressure is necessary, we have to support people by providing the time and necessary . . . resources to get better. But the work has to be close to the kids and the real problems that teachers describe. That's what we haven't done. We do millions of things that stop short of helping the teacher in his or her classroom. When teachers learn more, students will do better. There is no shortcut here.

Administrators under intense pressure may find it hard to allow professional development to unfold slowly, but it must in order to achieve deep, lasting change. To quote Fullan again, remember that "you can't mandate what matters" (1993, 21). Mandating rigid methods with even more rigid deadlines accomplishes nothing. Improved, focused teaching emerges slowly, with flexible leadership, and increased student learning is the ultimate and most precious benefit.

Phil Schlechty (1993) has identified five roles educators play when school restructuring begins, and these roles apply to staff development as well. The five types of people to look out for on your journey as a staff development leader are trailblazers, pioneers, settlers, stay-at-homes, and saboteurs.

Trailblazers want to go with you, wherever, in the name of adventure. They love novelty and enjoy taking risks. They personalize their vision and sometimes see obstacles as personal threats. They work well whether or not there is "proof" of an innovation's effectiveness. Trailblazers thrive when they are treated with latitude and unconventional support. They must sometimes be reminded that the goal is a shared vision and a community (not individual) quest. Trailblazers need to be sent to professional conferences so they remain motivated and can network with their trailblazer peers. These are your high-energy, straight-talking folks (most of the time), and they can sometimes rub people the wrong way. You'll meet one such trailblazer, Tracy Bailey, in later chapters.

Pioneers are willing to take risks and have many of the same needs as trailblazers. Cautious pioneers need assurance, though, that the trip is worth making. They like to read stories about trailblazers who have been successful and hear from such leaders in presentations or on video. Together, trailblazers and pioneers provide the two types of leadership that can get the other folks moving. The wise staff development facilitator identifies trailblazers and pioneers early on and uses them as cofacilitators. I have been a trailblazer before, and now I think I'm a tired trailblazer—or, in other words, a pioneer. I have become more cautious and take longer to commit to a change now. I find I need more information from successful trailblazers before I start out on the journey.

Settlers need maps. They are bold at times but not really adventurous. Others have to persuade them to join up. They will come along, as long as they know they can do what they are asked, and as long as they know the mission is worthwhile. These are the folks that don't like the fad of the moment waves that often roll through schools. They thrive with systematic training, coaching, and protection from negative consequences if they fail. If settlers become disheartened, skillful administrators, trailblazers, and pioneers must coax them into persevering. You will meet Emily Morton in chapter 2; I would characterize her as a settler.

The stay-at-homes often receive a lot of attention early in a change movement. They do not want to come along. They will endure what is known and comfortable even if it does not work. Schlechty encourages benign neglect of stay-at-homes, at least early in the change process. They do not necessarily hinder others from changing, and, as Schlechty notes, "Many stay-at-homes stay . . . because they truly love the place" (1993). You will read some written feedback that I have provided to stay-at-homes to get them to reconsider their methods later in the book.

The saboteurs are a different group entirely. Not only do they want to stay at home, they also want to stop change in its tracks. Ironically, they have many of the same qualities as trailblazers (risk-taking, etc.). Schlechty says that saboteurs need to be brought inside the group to be better monitored. On the periphery or in exclusion, they are dangerous. They can be quite disruptive, but if the skillful leader really tries to listen to them, much can be gleaned from their comments. Even if they don't come around in the end, they may limit or stop their sabotaging behavior, and this alone will increase the chances of success.

Researcher and educator Linda Darling-Hammond summarizes the big ideas in teacher learning very well:

> Good settings for teacher learning . . . provide lots of opportunities for research and inquiry, for trying and testing, for talking about and evaluating the results of learning and teaching. The "rub between theory and practice" (Miller and Silvernail 1994) occurs most productively when questions arise in the context of real students and work in progress, and where research and disciplined inquiry are also at hand (http://www.ascd.org/readingroom/edlead/9802/darlinghammondhtml [accessed 27 June 2003]).

Teachers must develop authentic questions within the context of their daily work. These authentic questions are the foundation of meaningful professional development. We can no longer open up teachers' heads and pour in knowledge any more than we can do this with the children in our schools.

STORIES: WHY THIS BOOK?

This book is about teaching who we are, from a unified sense of self. It's about viewing teaching from a researcher's stance, helping teachers find their questions and possible answers. In a spirit of questioning, learning, and growing, I am writing this book in order to spark conversations about making professional development for teachers more powerful. Playwright George Bernard Shaw is often quoted as saying: "Some people see things as they are and ask 'why?' I dream of things that never were, and ask 'why not?'" Educators' conversations must start addressing the "why not?" more than the "why?" Why not involve teachers in effective professional development from day one of their careers? Why not provide inservice that adds to the overall richness of one's life? Why not invest time, energy, and money in teacher learning to positively impact student learning?

After seventeen years as an educator and with the splendidly varied experiences I've had, I've come to realize that the time is now to help teachers change deeply. We can do this by using processes that are adaptable to any setting and any time in one's career, in addition to having both personal and professional merit.

The essence of this book is inquiry, reflection, discussion, and experimentation—all in the name of improving education for teachers, which in turn benefits students immeasurably. You will meet a few of the dynamic teachers I've had the pleasure to instruct and to learn from: some trailblazers, some pioneers, some settlers, even a couple of stay-at-homes and saboteurs. You'll see them in action through transcripts. You'll read excerpts from their teaching journals and will see some of the written feedback I've provided to them as I have observed in their classrooms. You will be riding along for part of my teaching–learning journey, and I hope you will consider the time invested a pleasurable part of your own travel.

As Marcel Proust once said, "The real art of discovery consists not in finding new lands, but in seeing with new eyes." I hope you will read about familiar lands in this book, but I also hope you will see some of the terrain with new eyes.

Read. Reflect. Question. Share with a colleague. Enjoy.

RESPONSE QUESTIONS FOR CHAPTER 1

1. Think about a recent staff development session you attended or led. What was good about it? What would you change if you could?

2. Who are the trailblazers, pioneers, settlers, stay-at-homes, and saboteurs in your current work situation? If I were a staff development consultant coming to your site to work with you and this group, what advice would you have for me? How can you best heed that advice yourself in working with them?

CHAPTER 2

An Inside-Out Model of Staff Development

"Out there things can happen and frequently do to people as brainy and footsy as you. And when things start to happen, don't worry, don't stew. Just go right along. *You'll* start happening too."

—Dr. Seuss in *Oh! The Places You'll Go*

"Teachers (individually and collectively) must develop the habits and skills of continuous inquiry and learning, always seeking new ideas inside and outside their own settings."

—Michael Fullan in *Change Forces:
Probing the Depths of Educational Reform*

Human beings are wonderfully multifaceted. We are at once emotional and intellectual, spiritual and earthly, introspective and social.

Teachers, too, of course, exhibit these marvelously paradoxical traits. What sets teachers apart from the rest of the general population, however, is that teachers are in the business of learning. They are charged with orchestrating learning every day. While this endeavor may seem to some folks a wholly intellectual pursuit, *it is not.* A teacher must work not only from her head but from her heart as well.

In order to be an effective teacher, one cannot be disconnected emotionally from self, subject matter, or students. There is an element of personal investment that must exist or the teaching of subject matter becomes rote, lifeless—a mere façade. As Parker Palmer (1997) notes, "Teaching, like any truly human activity, emerges from one's inwardness, for better or worse" (http://www.mcli.dist.maricopa.edu/fsd/afc99/articles/heartof.html [accessed 30 September 2003]).

With this concept of "inwardness" in mind, I reiterate: *professional development for teachers must change.*

In order for staff development to be meaningful and to result in positive growth, it must have an "inside-out" nature. All the legislative directives, standardized tests, and bureaucratic red tape do practically nothing to directly change the most important factor in the classroom: the teacher's ability to connect with students and to facilitate powerful learning experiences. Concurring with Palmer, I believe we need to "understand that inner work is as real as outer work and involves skills one can develop, skills like journaling, reflective reading, . . . friendship, [and] meditation" (2000, 91).

Professional development that enhances teacher effectiveness must contain a prudent combination of inner and outer work. One of the preeminent researchers in the area of teacher quality and professional development is Linda Darling-Hammond, currently of Stanford University. In her study "Teacher Quality and Student Achievement: A Review of State Policy Evidence" (http://epaa.asu.edu/epaa/v8n1), Darling-Hammond concludes that "policies adopted by states regarding teacher education, licensing, hiring, and professional development may make an important difference in the qualifications and capacities teachers bring to their work" (2000, 2). She cites numerous studies that support these two assertions: teacher effectiveness is a strong determinant of differences in student learning, outweighing other factors like class size; and students assigned to several ineffective teachers sequentially have lower achievement gains than those assigned to several effective teachers sequentially. It follows, then, that all educators should be concerned about giving teachers tools to be more effective so that students will learn more. Darling-Hammond notes that successful teachers are those who are able to use a wide range of teaching strategies and interaction styles (2000, 11). Where do teachers learn and refine these strategies in the course of their careers? Perhaps in high-quality staff development offerings, including graduate education courses, which have traditionally been more theoretical than practical. She ends her report with the following statement: "Over the next decade . . . policymakers interested in helping students meet higher learning standards may want to consider how investments in teacher quality, along with other reforms, can assist them in achieving their goals" (2000, 38). We are one-third of the way through that decade as I write this. While emphasis has been placed on testing and accountability mechanisms, we cannot forget to invest in the humans in the system—the teachers who are charged with orchestrating increasingly complex and challenging learning experiences for their students. These human investments cost very little but yield a substantial return.

From many directions, the implications are clear. Effective professional development must engage the hearts and heads of educators in order to keep teachers engaged in active learning and thereby help students achieve.

Ask any good teacher why he went into the field, and somewhere in the answer you'll hear reference to liking young people or wanting to share the love of a subject area with others. I've yet to hear a competent, satisfied teacher say, "I wanted to teach because I could earn approximately $10.50 an hour and have exactly twenty-five unencumbered vacation days per year." Overwhelmingly, teachers go into teaching for what Palmer (1997) calls "reasons of the heart"; most stay in it or leave it for the very same reasons. For example, Ann Twigg, an exemplary, passionate teacher in her seventeenth year of teaching, shows uncharacteristic dissatisfaction in a reflective journal entry written for a graduate course:

> If I only felt good about other things. I'm still tremendously frustrated by my feelings concerning standardized testing. . . . Sometimes the angry feelings turn into apathetic shrugs; I never thought I wouldn't care about what I'm doing. I've been waking up prior to the alarm but not wanting to get out of bed just because I don't want to face another day at school. Who wants a teacher with these feelings? I wouldn't. Of course, my teacher self takes over by the time I arrive in the parking lot, and I give it my all. And sometimes I'm not satisfied with that! Where's the fun?

Ann asks, "Where's the fun?" Certainly not in professional development in many instances. As educators, we have all sat for hours and listened to an out-of-town consultant drone on and on about something we care little about. This is not effective inservice.

Effective professional development must first engage the heart of the teacher. It must be inviting. From the onset, it must be comfortable. Food often helps and sets a tone of nourishing both the body and the mind. Really, are you to able concentrate when hungry or tired without a little pick-me-up? Remember Abraham Maslow's hierarchy of needs from all your beginning education courses: a person must feel safe and have basic needs met (food, clothing, shelter) before being able to attend to more cerebral matters. This is basic psychology and physiology but is often forgotten as a prerequisite for meaningful adult instruction.

Ideally, the participants in any inservice should have some kind of relationship with each other and some sort of familiarity with the facilitator. If these kinds of connections don't exist, relationships must be built within the first few minutes. If a staff development facilitator is new to the group and doesn't use a feel-good, "let's get to know each other" technique in the very first session, that's reason to discontinue a contractual agreement with him. We teachers often say students have to know how much we care before they care how much we know; the same should apply to all teachers of teachers, be they administrators, graduate school instructors, or professional consultants. As testament to establishing a comfortable learning atmosphere for teachers, read what several teachers had to say after just one day in the Coastal Area Writing Project's (CAWP) 2000 summer institute:

"The group is so responsive to everything everybody says and is very supportive. Good group dynamics. It's nice not to have to drive for lunch!"

"I enjoyed the . . . format of the day. . . . Thank you for the delicious food and enjoyable day."

"I like the variety of activities and learning in a safe environment. It is wonderful to be able to nourish the different 'selves' within us (that we sometimes neglect)."

"I like the laid-back atmosphere. You don't feel intimidated to share and . . . feel free to share if you want to."

"Today was wonderful. I am amazed at the community that has formed."

"I really like everything I have encountered so far. . . . Thank you most of all for the positive, affirming attitudes of our two 'teachers.' PS Great meal—thank you!"

The teachers appreciated the atmosphere that was created, which included supportive instructor attitudes, a variety of activities, and lunch supplied by a group of participants. Basic emotional and physical needs were met first, and then some intellectual work was attended to. On the second day of the course, the emotional and physical needs were not neglected, but more intellectual work was undertaken. Moving from a safe, inviting climate to serious, cognitive work is easier when a group has days or weeks to be together, but it is not impossible even in a one-hour inservice. (See appendix A for tips on adding an inside-out component to any type of meeting.)

In any inservice, once everyone is alert and fed and a comfortable working relationship has been established, *then and only then* should the group proceed to more intellectual pursuits. Effective professional development must first establish the "inside" climate and then progress outward into examining the topics at hand through such methods as presentation, dialogue, research, writing, planning, and coaching. Teachers must be involved in taking in information, manipulating it in various ways, and interacting with colleagues before putting learning "outside" into a repertoire of classroom practice. One teacher commented, upon completing the Writing Project summer course: "To my school classroom: what amazing ideas! Enthusiasm, strategies, writing/ art journals. My classroom will now be a studio. I will conference about writing and celebrate more. I will take a feeling of support, friendship, and validation from my Writing Project family." Another teacher in the same group said, "As a result of taking this class, I will be: offering more diversity in activities; offering more choices for my students; . . . offering a venue that allows for more creativity; letting students form the questions they want answers for; letting students work in groups where talking is allowed. The list goes on and on!" If a course or workshop has been productive, the learning continues because it has directly addressed the realities of the classroom. In Frank Clark's e-mail to me Nov. 15, 2001, he demonstrates continued learning and application: "It is with a great deal of relief that I see my Writing Project ideas . . . take hold in my classroom. A lot of the problem was my hesitation in implementing the ideas. They were great for my writing and enjoyable at the same time. To take it that extra step [of implementation] was monumental!"

Support for new practices must continue long after any inservice offering is complete. For those who have been National Writing Project fellows, continuity meetings are held at least once a year to offer this kind of support, and past fellows often reconnect at professional conferences and various district or regional meetings. Graduate programs for teachers as a rule do not have the same long-term support component, so instructors should explore creative ways to create such follow-up. A school or district's staff development plan must address how to sustain changes that teachers make as a result of attending inservice. It helps if all the inservice offerings tie into a larger, shared organizational goal coherently, and if not, the leaders should reconsider their plans.

The participants in a session I led at the 2002 National Association of Secondary School Principals Annual Convention brainstormed this list of words related to effective professional development: timely, relevant, pertinent, meaningful, practical, active, hands-on, choice, buy-in, accountability, application, classroom, cost-effective, collaborative, and follow-through. The teachers in the Coastal Area Writing Project's summer institute in 2000 generated this list of qualities of effective staff development, based on the experience they had just completed: an inviting learning environment; learner-centered work and learner choice; immersion in learning; large blocks of time to read, write, talk, and do research; receiving peer and teacher response; learning specific strategies; having reflection time; the valuing of community and process. The teachers also brainstormed a list of what they hated about a "bad" professional development simulation and previous ineffective inservices they had attended: a rush to cover prescribed material; no response time or time to talk with peers or instructor; "canned" content; lack of respect for student input; a hostile, sterile learning environment; teacher-centered learning; lack of choice and no individualization; no talking or collaboration among students. The two groups, which included a total of over 100 educators, seem to have compatible visions. If this is so, why do administrators *at all levels* persist in offering inservices that do not meet the needs of teachers? Why can't teachers and administrators join forces and improve inservice for all?

To review, by inside-out staff development I mean:

- Process is emphasized over product, and the continuous learning of teachers is valued above all.

- Staff developers honor their audiences by seeking to make them comfortable, honoring their basic physical and emotional needs, planning relevant and engaging tasks, and knowing the professionals with whom they work as individuals, not merely as stereotypes, groups, or categories.
- Teachers reflect on their learning as well as their teaching and try to reignite the passion that brought them into the profession.
- Teachers inquire into their own practice and seek to improve.
- Teachers process new information, demonstrate their learning, and collaborate with colleagues in a larger network of competent professionals.
- Supervisors not only observe the end result (improved teaching) but also participate in the process of inquiry, reflection, and collegiality. They do this without exerting authority only for authority's sake and without being unnecessarily punitive toward those whom they supervise. Just like the teachers involved, administrators must agree to be imperfect learners, too.

This inside-out model parallels scientific inquiry. Teachers often have "wonderings," similar to a scientist's hypotheses. For example, a teacher may think, "I wonder why my students still have trouble with capitalizing proper nouns. What can I do to teach this concept differently and help them learn better?" The general hypothesis follows: If I teach a new strategy, I expect to see improvement in the capitalization of proper nouns.

Next, the teacher calls upon others by opening a professional book, asking a staff development consultant, colleague, or supervisor, or frantically searching the Internet for exemplary lesson plans. She then learns about a myriad of different ways to teach capitalization of proper nouns. She sorts through all this information, chooses wisely, and enacts a new method or two in the classroom.

It's time for the laboratory work. She must step back from herself a bit and try to reflect in action and on action (Schön 1983). She observes the students as they grapple with the concept in a new way. Either the experiment is successful, or it fails and puts the teacher-scientist back to square one. If the new strategy did not work and produced the same results as before (meaning the students still don't capitalize proper nouns with high accuracy), she must study the results and set up a new experiment. This point is where coaching and collegiality enter. If the teacher tried something that did not work, it's very easy for her simply to quit and go on to the next skill, the next chapter, or whatever has to be covered according to the sacred curriculum document disseminated from on high. But the kids still don't know how to capitalize proper nouns correctly! The teacher must try, try again, even though in many ways it seems more expedient to leave half the kids in the dust and zoom on to the next topic.

Skillful staff development facilitators, curriculum coaches, and administrators must encourage this form of inquiry and must value depth over breadth—a hard task in our American culture of quick-fix remedies. Encouraging questions, reteaching, and close observation of students as a way of life in the classroom will have lasting benefits for both the adults and the children in the building. Observe the growth displayed by high school English teacher Sharon Cunningham in a journal entry completed at a Writing Project continuity meeting held months after the summer graduate course: "I have totally reconsidered my teaching approaches, techniques, and focus of instruction. Previously I was consumed with meeting district and state standards. Now I am stretching. . . . I am constantly trying to envision new ideas for inspirational instruction. . . . I am confident that my main goal will be achieved. My students will find 'voice.'"

We must engage the heads of educators to keep them inquiring, researching, and trying different techniques to produce real learning. We must engage the hearts of educators so that they remember why they loved teaching from the start: because they love igniting the fires of learning in younger people.

STORIES: FIVE PRACTITIONERS CALL FOR INSIDE-OUT STAFF DEVELOPMENT

Ms. Meier

Gretchen Meier is a twenty-eight-year-old teacher of middle school language arts and social studies. She has taught for five years and says she has never thought about leaving the profession but admits she is "still in the honeymoon phase a bit."

When asked why she chose teaching, Gretchen says she thought she always knew that's what she would do. "I . . . played school with my friends and I was always the teacher. My mom still has 'worksheets' I would make up and notebooks I would use as my 'gradebook.' My favorite part of the day was reading . . . and it just seemed like teaching is where I belonged. No one seemed surprised at all when I applied to a school of education. I just feel I belong up in front of a bunch of kids."

As far as effective professional development goes, Gretchen says that the Writing Project helped her. She participated in the summer institute and, within the following two years, three graduate courses cotaught by the local Writing Project and Coastal Carolina University. She calls these experiences "useful." To elaborate, she says:

> I think the fact that I love being a student as well as a teacher has been the biggest thing for me. I love sitting in classes and learning and sharing ideas. I think that is more useful than any theory class that can be offered. I'd be willing to spend my time on things that I can gain . . . practical things and ideas from. Don't waste my time on things I don't need. And more than anything, [I appreciate] the opportunity to meet teachers and work with them. That is probably number one and where most of my most fabulous ideas have come from. . . . I think sometimes when I sit through things that don't have direct application to me, I get uninterested very quickly and that hurts me.

You may be thinking that Gretchen sounds like students in your school. If you teach high school students, she may, because immediacy and relevance are key components of adult learning theory, and high school students already begin to question why they have to do certain tasks. Gretchen demands immediate application of what she is learning in staff development and/or graduate classes; most teachers do. Should they expect less?

Gretchen also reminds supervisors not to forget using humor and lightheartedness to support teachers. She explains:

> Some days the only way I get through the day is to just sit down and laugh my ass off, and that's not always so easy. We give so much of ourselves . . . and a lot of times it feels like we get nothing back. Well,

when you get nothing back then obviously a part of you is lost. Someone needs to give it back, and 99 percent of the time it is one of your coworkers. . . . People who don't teach just will never quite get what it's like. Now perhaps this is just me, but find a silly and fun way to reward [the teachers] and show [them] that they are appreciated. I think that is the reason why there is a problem with teacher retention—we work our asses off and get very little in return. Sometimes you need more than the intrinsic value of knowing you have imparted . . . knowledge to our youth. Give out silly awards to a few staff members each month, stick a candy bar in each person's mailbox every so often, do something that is a bit silly but fun. There are so many teachers that work so hard . . . and do a great job but are too meek to make themselves recognizable; this way everyone gets a little something. This would develop a staff more than anything because it develops a STAFF, a group of people who work together for a common goal. We work so hard to make our classes fun for our kids and make them want to come to school each day. The same needs to be done for teachers.

Strong words for strong feelings. Gretchen points out one of the biggest complaints teachers have—they do not feel appreciated by their bosses. One of the best (and free) ways to show appreciation is to offer kudos in some kind of regular format—in a school newsletter, over the intercom or school TV news program, or at faculty meetings. When the principal makes a point to recognize special things teachers do in a proud, public manner, teachers feel that people other than their students value their work. Also, the healthy values of laughter are well documented. Sharing a joke or humorous anecdote at the beginning of a typical faculty meeting or planning an activity that allows some of the "clowns" on the faculty to shine will go a long way in keeping stress to a minimum.

When asked what has hindered her own professional development, Gretchen cites finances as one reason, noting the high cost of graduate courses. She also comments on why teachers may get exasperated enough to leave the field:

It is the political junk that irritates me, and I can see why people would leave. As teachers I think we are due a whole lot more respect than what we are given and [are] dealt out a whole lot more to deal with than what most people realize. . . . Respect my job and respect my time. Don't make me do things that are a waste. Don't make me sit and do silly things in staff development. Give me what I need and let me work in my room and with other teachers to make me a better teacher.

Gretchen, like most teachers, is a willing collaborator only if she sees value in the collaboration. This is an important point. Collaboration can be neither random nor forced. It must also have direct application to one's classroom teaching in order for it to be valuable.

She says that she has most enjoyed professional development sessions she herself has chosen, like working with nationally known literacy consultants. "This is what districts need to bring in," Gretchen recommends. She continues, "Bad professional development is done by people who haven't seen the inside of a classroom in a long time, [and] . . . I hate theory. I hate things that don't have direct impact on me. . . . I have kids who can't spell, who can't write, and can't read. Tell me how to fix that. Don't tell me how to manage a classroom using coloring books and singing songs. I need real, tried and true methods, not someone standing on a stage who never even taught or who hasn't met a teenager since they themselves were a teenager."

In the interview I conducted with her, Gretchen reiterated some of my points movingly. Teachers value respect, choice, relevance, and collaboration with competent peers. They devalue what is perceived as distant, unrealistic theory. Teachers are resistant when they feel the changes they are asked to make are handed out in a dictatorial fashion or by people who do not know the "in the trenches" realities.

Mrs. Bailey

Tracy Bailey is a twenty-eight-year-old former high school English and journalism teacher, who is now a full-time mother and part-time graduate student and educational consultant. She taught for over six years and says she "initially got into teaching out of a sense of responsibility." She clarifies this statement further:

One day as I sat in my Introduction to Education class, I realized how important it would be for young African-American students to see other

African-Americans who had succeeded in the area of education. . . . [H]ow fortunate I was to have been blessed with such positive role models throughout my education. I wanted to give that back in a way that no other students in my class could. I was the only African-American in the room. It was at that precise moment that the seed was planted. . . .

Tracy speaks to the "teaching who we are" concept (Palmer 1997) as she continues:

Over the years I have been blessed with mentors, role models, and sister-friends who take the time to see more than just a teacher, but look me in the eye and see a human being. I've had many opportunities to share my inspirations and struggles in safe, [nonthreatening] environments. . . . So it has been relationship and fellowship that have sustained and supported me as a learner and professional.

Tracy says that if anything has hindered her professional growth, it has been her own competitive spirit and tendency to become consumed by work. These aspects of her personality often led her to heated discussions with colleagues: "I often found myself in the position of defending my core philosophies about teaching, as they conflicted with those of my colleagues." She says she had to go outside her own school to find like-minded teachers, and this sometimes seemed unsupportive to others. She specifically cites being a "trailblazer" and dealing with abundant paperwork as things that sapped her energy, particularly as she got married and began to contemplate having children. She shows her feelings of a lack of self-efficacy when she adds, "I could never seem to juggle everything successfully."

Why did a trailblazer with such strong convictions leave education? "I left teaching in order to give myself time and space to learn how to balance my passion for teaching and learning with my passion for my family," she answers.

Tracy did find some good professional development along the way. She feels teachers learn best in "a [nonrestrictive], active environment. I loved the Horry County Schools Integrated Thematic Instruction Model Teaching week, where I was able to see techniques first-hand, ask questions, then implement new strategies." Tracy was also an active participant in the Writing Project and is now a frequent presenter for its classes and institutes. As for "bad" professional development, Tracy echoes Gretchen when she says it "keeps me in my seat too long and is more about theory than practice."

Again, we see from Tracy's comments that teachers need relevant professional learning, collegial dialogue, and recognition of the person behind the teaching. Another dimension Tracy touches upon in her comments is the demonstration of successful techniques, perhaps followed up with coaching from a mentor.

Mrs. Twigg

Ann Twigg is a thirty-eight-year-old high school English teacher in her seventeenth year of teaching. She is married with two daughters and is very involved in her church, community, and extracurricular activities at her school.

When I asked Ann why she chose teaching, she replied:

> Wow, what a question! I've always felt the need to help others and wanted to make a difference in the world. Where else could I touch so many souls? My mom didn't work when we were small but went back to school when my youngest sister was four. She became a teacher's assistant and worked with special education for years. I remember her buying a boy a pair of shoes because his family couldn't afford much. I remember thinking, "I want to do that for somebody."

In this answer, Ann exhibits many of the same "reasons of the heart" (Palmer 1997) as other teachers: a sense of service or duty, the feeling of making a difference, and emulating a role model, like a parent or teacher.

Ann knows what helps her grow professionally. She continues: "Most of my support has come from the Coastal Area Writing Project. The classes and workshops offered through this special program have helped shape me into the individual and teacher I am today. The people I met have become close friends and colleagues. The ideas and strategies shared have become treasures."

Notice that Ann did not separate her "teacher-self" from her "personal self" in that answer: she said the "individual and teacher I am today." She also notes support from her family, saying, "My husband believes in me. My daughters admire me. That's an extra plus. I wouldn't make it otherwise." Indeed, many teachers, particularly those who are mothers, cite a lack of family time or undue stress on the family as a main reason for leaving teaching. It is crucial for administrators to honor the desire that all teachers have to spend time with families, no matter what form those families may take: spouses, children, siblings, roommates, heterosexual or homosexual companions, aging parents, close friends, beloved pets, and extended family. Contrary to popular practice, even young, single teachers (who are often overburdened with extracurricular responsibilities) need quality time with family and must have it in order to stay positive about teaching.

What kills the joy of teaching for Ann? "The district and state mandates that are required drown my passion," she says. "Some of what is required is not what is best for the students. I am saddened when I have to teach to a test. [Also,] teachers are pressured to be parents. The accountability factor is too high considering all the obstacles we face." Ann is a frequent presenter for her school district and was even featured in a training videotape as a model high school English teacher. She has completed her master's degree and an additional thirty graduate hours and has considered obtaining her National Board certificate. However, she cites the abundant paperwork required for the certification as a hindrance and also feels the process lacks integrity:

> I applied but withdrew a little over a month before the due date. I was too busy being a teacher (state presentation preparation, lesson plans, grading, extracurricular activities) to complete the additional paperwork. The stress was hurting my students, family, and me. It was also hard to complete the process [knowing that] I don't believe a group of strangers can read over a mountain of papers, watch a videotape, assess a written test, and determine a teacher worthy of the certification. Where's the heart? Isn't that what teaching is all about?

Eloquent point, Ann. Ineffective professional development for teachers lacks heart. So does much of the work teachers are required to do for advanced certification and salary increases. Many times, the credits are earned in ways that do not address the core of teaching: the passion for learning, the joy in working with students, the excitement of sharing compelling subject matter.

Like many others, Ann has thought about leaving the field. It is hard to imagine how much damage has been done over the years to countless students because effective teachers like Ann have stopped teaching. Why has she considered it? "The stress has become overwhelming," she begins. "There is too much testing and too many strangers telling us what is best for our students. Much of the paperwork has no meaning. However, I don't know of another thing that . . . rewards as teaching does, despite all the frustration."

When giving advice about what to do to orchestrate good professional development, Ann feels it's important for like-minded peers to be able to collaborate and cites the Writing Project as very influential in her own growth. By participating in the Writing Project, she says she met "so many teachers who share the same educational philosophy with me." As for bad professional development, she cites "some of the teacher meetings," including general faculty meetings as well as additional training sessions for testing, technology, and other district and school mandates. She adds, "Sometimes we meet just for the sake of meeting. Many of us have so many other things we could be doing in our classrooms." This sentiment is clear testament to why isolation in teaching has been perpetuated for decades. Well-meaning administrators plan meetings that teachers deem irrelevant. Teachers become upset, thinking about all the other tasks they could be completing that more directly touch students. Some veteran teachers choose to tune out most everything done in mass meetings and learn to keep more and more to themselves. This "sealing off" is unproductive and results in stagnation for teacher, students, and the school as a learning organization.

Ms. Morton

Emily Morton is a fifty-three-year-old middle school language arts teacher beginning her thirtieth year of teaching. She taught elementary school for several years just prior to specializing in middle school language arts in 1989. She lives with her daughter and two-year-old grandchild.

Emily says she went into teaching because she really thought there were only two career avenues open to her—teaching and nursing. However, she doesn't think she would do something else now even if she could go back in time and choose again. She says she would, however, like to start teaching again with the knowledge she has now. Also, she notes a subconscious desire to be dramatic. In teaching, she has a captive audience and finds she can "express [herself] in a dramatic way." This dramatic side, which she says she never shows even her own family, is one way she feels she exercises creativity in her vocation, and she thinks creativity is one of the qualities of teaching that has kept her in it for so long.

Emily finds teaching self-fulfilling. She adds that it is "not particularly consistent," but also says that she is deeply touched when students she taught years ago come up to her and are still able to articulate what they learned from her. One sixth-grade student, who is now married, told Emily that she still has the journal she wrote in Emily's class years ago and keeps it in a dresser drawer. This encounter was very special to Emily, because it proves "there are those who have benefited from my teaching." Most teachers I've worked with cite this sense of making a difference when they talk about why they remain in the profession.

Emily recently completed a graduate course in literacy and thinks it was the best she has ever taken. When asked what made it so effective, she says: "In teaching, sometimes I feel like I'm on a treadmill. In this course, I got to say, 'Oh yeah, it's okay to do this!'" Emily found affirmation for using strategies she already employed when these strategies were highlighted by the instructor and also appeared in the professional reading. For example, she remembers reading one sentence in the course textbook about a student saying no teacher had ever asked him what he thought before. Emily says, "That sentence won't leave me alone!" She has remembered to repeatedly ask her students "What do you think about that?" ever since reading the article, although she was doing this before, too. The article seemed to remind her of the importance of encouraging critical thinking, and she has focused on doing just that even more directly since she took the course.

The course, overall, had "the most practical approach I've ever seen," Emily raves. "Now I don't feel like I'm floundering. I feel much more organized," she adds, when discussing all the strategies she has fine-tuned or implemented as a result of completing the course.

One of the features of the literacy course, which was, incidentally, taught by a Writing Project alumnus, was to begin every class session with journal-writing time. The instructor provided an interesting professional article to which participants responded. I've also used this technique to begin after-school meetings or classes and have found it quite effective, as it allows time for all to arrive. Those who arrive early may choose to focus immediately or to ease in to their work in order to release some of the stresses of the day. Those who arrive later feel pressured to get to work but are not excluded from the first activity of the class simply because they were a few minutes behind others.

Emily realizes she is a more self-directed learner than a collaborative one and says that she grows impatient with those teachers who want to discuss personal issues as part of a graduate course or inservice. She prefers to focus on the work at hand. As part of her independent learning nature, she says she likes to observe in classrooms to see strategies in action or to watch an effective lesson. This immersion is something she feels she can take directly back with her and incorporate. For example, she has made two school visits this year. At both schools, she observed Socratic seminars being used effectively and wants to adapt them for her classes. She is committed to trying the seminars in future lessons.

Emily also learns from trial and error and on-site coaching. This year, I have had the opportunity to be the language arts coach at her school. When a lesson does not go as smoothly as expected, Emily seeks me out for advice. Sometimes I go observe what she is doing and make suggestions. She finds this kind of give and take helpful. Also, at times, I have taught demonstration lessons in her classes at her request. Knowing that she learns a great deal from seeing another teacher teach, this is an important component of her professional development, and I always strive to execute exemplary lessons.

Emily says she has no plans to retire soon and looks forward to using things learned from the graduate course and from my coaching in her teaching in the coming years. She admits she expects all sorts of "bandwagons" and "fads" to come into focus and then move out again, as they seem to do every year, but she feels equipped to handle the disruptions.

Mrs. Hart

Ruby Hart is a forty-seven-year-old teacher who came into the field in an untraditional way and left after about eleven years. She began teaching after working as a permanent substitute at an elementary school for five years.

> I worked all different grade levels including all special [education] classes. If I didn't have a class, I worked in the office with the principal learning about how a school works. I thought to myself, "I can do this. I can teach." So I went to school in the evenings after work. The job was perfect for me. I liked the fact that I changed classes on a regular basis, so I knew all the students and staff. The days and years flew by and before you [knew] it, it was time to leave to complete . . . college.

Ruby has taught a variety of grades. She began as a resource teacher because "they needed one badly," as she says. She continues with her story:

> Since I had no special education credits I moved to second grade, . . . which I taught for four years. While I was teaching second grade, I decided to get my masters in . . . reading. I thought of those students in resource and how nothing in college prepared me to deal with their learning problems, so I wanted to specialize in teaching reading. After I received my masters, I was offered the job as a reading specialist. I was a . . . floater for two years. . . . I worked with second through fifth grade. During my last year at that school we had to [let a teacher go] due to low enrollment. Three weeks into the school year, a fifth grade teacher was transferred so I inherited her class. It was a good year. I was glad to have a room again and I enjoyed the age and subject matter. In class were several students I had taught in second grade, so they are really special to me. When these students left I decided to transfer.

Ruby then transferred to a smaller, more rural, poorer, segregated school. The district was building a new school nearby to finally comply with integration legislation. Of this period, she says:

I taught third grade for three years, and then was offered another reading specialist job. By then, I had earned thirty hours above my masters. This time I was not the lone reading specialist. There were three of us and each of us had a nice room. You would think it would have been a perfect year, but it was far from it. Because our school had received below-average [ratings] on our [state] report card, the school climate changed dramatically. The principal was scared she would lose her job . . . her whole personality changed. Teachers were overworked . . . and very irritable. I didn't have a homeroom and so I was overloaded with responsibility. September 11 happened that year, adding to the stress.

Prior to the year described above, Ruby had participated in the Writing Project and had found it professionally worthwhile. She took another course during the school year, which she says "was being taught, in my eyes, very poorly." She continues:

I was spoiled by the Coastal Area Writing Project's fast-paced, motivating style. [T]he quantity (and quality) of like-minded teachers was not present in this class . . . I was dying. . . . I felt like jumping up and teaching it myself it was so badly taught. It was slow, poorly planned, and some of it was just plain bad information. We didn't have as much input as we could have given. The teacher droned on and on like a pesky mosquito. At one point, I left, but I returned, thinking it's just me, my attitude. I returned to more of the same, so I dropped the class.

Ruby has articulated much about what makes for bad professional development: slow pacing, misinformation, ineffective instructors, unmotivated classmates, and disorganization or poor planning. After having experienced good professional development in the previous summer's Writing Project and then in its continuity meetings, she was totally unprepared for a course that stood in such stark contrast and literally shocked her sensibilities.

At the end of that year Ruby resigned, "for a long list of professional and personal reasons." Her resignation letter was one sentence: "In order to pursue another avenue of education, I resign for the year 2002–2003." She wanted to take "a mid-career break and pick up a couple of homebound students," she says. She also says that her health was not good and she needed rest.

Ruby traveled that summer, doing some camping out West. When she returned to South Carolina, she decided to pursue writing. Here's how she did it:

> I [e-mailed] the local newspaper to ask if they could use some teacher-voiced, research-based articles on education, just for the [personal] writing experience. I wanted to write about the big issues. Little did I know I was about to open a big can of political worms. I began writing articles, and in a few weeks, the editor gave me my own column. I wrote about [sensitive] national, state, and . . . local issues and how they affect our corner of the world. Teachers started calling me to tell me their problems, and I began writing about the plight of teachers in this county. The community was definitely reading. We changed three school board members in the November election. Teachers had a voice without being reprimanded, and they read [my articles] for entertainment and to learn something.

Ruby immersed herself in writing and says she found her style, voice, and humor. By her account, she had surely lost these in her last year of teaching. She says, "I enjoy the research and writing process so much. The Coastal Area Writing Project was the catalyst that caused me to enjoy being a writer. I always had the interest, but CAWP opened the doors wide for me to see the possibilities in writing."

Most teachers who complete the Writing Project do not leave teaching and become writers; actually, I'm sure less than one percent of them do! But Ruby discovered she was "living divided" (Palmer 1997) and could no longer do it. She had to leave teaching to want to return to it again in the future.

> Now I am at a terrible crossroads. I have accumulated sixteen years in the state retirement system, and I can't throw that away. I want to go back to work, but not in this county. I don't know if they want me back, with the changes that occurred. . . . I was painfully honest in my column . . . I would probably have to give up my column to work here again, and I'm not willing to give it up. I have applied in various other counties.

Ruby wants to teach again, although she notes that her goals have changed. "No longer do I want to be just an early childhood/reading specialist," she begins. "I am seeking something more. I have a few possibilities to explore. Who knows what the future holds for me? Writing has changed my life."

Ruby has been on an inside-out journey and is a changed person. Will she be a better teacher when she returns to the profession? In my opinion, you can count on it.

RESPONSE QUESTIONS FOR CHAPTER 2

1. What has been the most positive professional development experience you've ever had? What qualities made it so positive? How has it changed your teaching?
2. If you are still working in education, why have you stayed in the field? What can you do to minimize the negatives in order to stay enthusiastic about your profession?

CHAPTER 3

Inside-Out as a Learner

"You cannot teach a man anything. You can only help him find it within himself."

—Galileo

"What lies behind us and . . . before us are tiny matters compared to what lies within us."

—Ralph Waldo Emerson

Many veteran teachers have forgotten what it's like to be a student and active learner. License renewal requirements are often met through attending routine inservice offerings, most of which lack the components of deep reflection and sustained follow-up. Some novice teachers, fresh out of college, have been well trained in the traditional instructional methods that failed even them, yet they revert to these methods rapidly as they first enter the profession.

In my own teacher training—and unfortunately with many of the early-career teachers I now know—the idea of "teacher as manager" is still emphasized over "teacher as thinker." This attentiveness to rewards, punishments, and control above discovery, inquiry, and creativity has had an adverse effect on the education profession, making teachers sometimes mistrust themselves and turn to dry, prepackaged materials and lockstep, unfamiliar methods, when instead, designing their own strategies, finding comfortable, effective methods, and discovering new resources could prove exhilarating. They frequently look to managers to make decisions, fully accepting the hierarchical structure of education instead of looking inward and honoring their own various forms of creativity and intelligence.

Revitalizing one's creativity and intelligence can come from being a true student again. Educators need time to be students in several different ways. First, they benefit greatly from rediscovering their own learning preferences. They also benefit from reexperiencing subject matter from the student or "novice" stance instead of the teacher or "expert" one. This reexperiencing is an important component of inside-out staff development. Inside, we must examine our own attitudes, personality types, learning styles, and communication preferences. We then apply our new understandings twofold: to our own learning and to our work with students. Outside, we must engage in activities that require us to reawaken our learning selves. Being a student again creates greater empathy for students in our classrooms while deepening our understanding of subject matter.

Reminiscent of Parker Palmer's "we teach who we are" dictum once again, we teachers often fall back on processes that are most comfortable for us. If I am a highly verbal person and learn well through auditory methods, I may teach predominantly through lecture, discussion, and giving notes. If, on the other hand, I am a strongly kinesthetic person and learn well through hands-on or body movement methods, I probably incorporate physical activity, manipulatives, and simulations into instruction. Alas, my auditory preference learners are left behind or struggle to make sense of it all, just as the "body-smart" (Armstrong 1999) students fall behind in the highly verbal/auditory classroom.

Another topic related to the concept of teacher as learner is the concept of primary ignorance ("you don't know that you don't know"). Some teachers become stagnant, thinking they have nothing to learn, or are too tired or frustrated by the system to reengage themselves in the business of real learning. A few of these educators are classic examples of primary ignorance, not discovering new methods or purposefully ignoring updated information because they truly believe their old, comfortable ways are best. They do not entertain the notion that there is anything more effective out there, even if their methods are not reaching students. These are the folks who often complain about how different the kids are nowadays, how unsupportive the parents are, and how demanding the administration is, although they have not looked in the mirror and asked, "What could I do differently to produce different results?" The answer for this group of teachers is "nothing," which reflects primary ignorance. They are ignorant of what they are ignorant of—meaning they don't know what they are missing. For various reasons, they have not experienced another way and hold to their old methods. They are Phil Schlechty's stay-at-homes in the worst sense of the term, and must experience some kind of learning experience that brings about the epiphany that yes, there is another way!

Related to primary ignorance is Donald Schön's discussion of "overlearning." He notes that some teachers are "drawn into patterns of error [that they] cannot correct" (1983, 61). It is hard to correct one's own ineffective patterns if there is no true dialogue, collaboration, or reawakening of the student-like mind. Through experiencing learning from the student's perspective with the help of collaborative colleagues, teachers may identify their own unsuccessful teaching patterns. Rigidity in practice is then lessened. As high school social studies teacher Frank Clark wrote in a journal entry as part of a graduate education course: "Teachers can be such hypocrites! We ask students to do things we won't do ourselves. . . . It takes a good amount of time to change teaching habits, but now is the time to start." Frank wrote this after reflecting upon methods he had previously used to teach writing in his classes. He realized he had been using some techniques that weren't encouraging his students to invest in writing personally. How did he learn this important lesson? By being a struggling (but eventually successful) writer. He himself learned to write in new ways, an accomplishment that pushed him to be more invested not only in writing as a tool for learning but also in his teaching methods as well.

When pushed out of their comfort zones, teachers are fiery learners and often go far beyond what even they predicted or desired for themselves. I have seen reluctant English teachers become prolific readers, writers, and presenters in a period of a few short weeks in the Writing Project summer institute. I've seen unsure elementary school teachers turn into budding scientists using computer-based laboratories as part of a district's model teaching week. I've witnessed secondary math teachers squealing with delight as they learned how to use new graphing calculators as part of a district-wide standards piloting initiative. An inside, personal learning experience aligned with content to be taught is essential if a teacher is to reflect upon and improve instruction. In summary, being a student again is the first step in being a better teacher.

PERSONALITY AND INTELLECT: LOOKING INSIDE

Where to start? How do we begin to know ourselves better as adult learners, so that our teaching is enhanced? When working with adults, I like to delve into two facets of one's learning self: intellect and personality. The most useful frameworks I've found to help me in this regard are Howard Gardner's theory of multiple intelligences (MI) and the Myers-Briggs model of temperament.

Gardner is famous for identifying seven different kinds of intelligence in his book *Frames of Mind* (1983). Briefly, they are as follows: linguistic (sensitivity to the meaning and order of words); logical-mathematical (strength in logic and mathematical operations); musical (sensitivity to rhythm and the ability to appreciate and/or create music); visual-spatial (the ability to perceive the visual and physical world accurately); bodily-kinesthetic (the ability to use one's body in a skilled way); interpersonal (the ability to understand and interact well with others); and intrapersonal (a deep awareness of one's own spirituality and emotions). Since publication of that book, Gardner has identified an eighth intelligence, the naturalist, which consists of the ability to recognize and classify items in the physical (especially the natural) world (Checkley 1997). Charles Darwin is the epitome of a person strong in the naturalist intelligence.

Gardner's MI theory is useful when working with both students and teachers. As a staff development consultant, I ensure I provide for interpersonal and intrapersonal strengths in every inservice. I almost always use a form of written reflection, like a journal entry, entrance slip, or exit slip as an intrapersonal activity. I usually use a form of community circle (Gibbs 1994), pair-share, or other purposeful talking activity as well. When I taught high school English, my class periods were ninety minutes long. Each day's lesson plan incorporated some interpersonal or talking/sharing time, as well as a quieter, more reflective, intrapersonal time like silent reading or journal writing. In this way, different strengths were tapped into and everyone had a point in the lesson during which she felt most comfortable and was perhaps learning at her best.

I find the other intelligences a bit harder to honor, especially when working with adults. However, it's important to allow adults latitude in completing some of the tasks in any staff development setting. If the final product is to be a unit plan or performance assessment task, for instance, teachers could present their ideas to the group and be encouraged to use various presentation modes and attention-grabbing tactics. The more musically inclined may choose to develop an original song to deliver as part of the presentation. The strongly kinesthetic learners may perform some sort of skit, role-play, or tableaux. Those gifted in the visual-spatial intelligence may choose to make a poster, three-dimensional figure, or other work of art. The strongly linguistic and logical (and there are plenty of these folks in the teaching profession) will be able to present in just about any manner whether they are alone or in a group, although activities like skits or songs may make them uncomfortable. They should be allowed to shine as the master planners of the presentation, the narrators, or the recorders of information for the group.

As a presenter, one must think about presentation modes as well. Because I am highly linguistic and logical, I often like to lecture and must force myself to include drawing or other hands-on activities so that I'm getting my message across more effectively. It's easy for me to remember the interpersonal and intrapersonal activities but harder to include some of the other intelligences in a direct way. As I'm in the final planning stages for any workshop or presentation, I push myself to address at least one of the intelligences that I may have slighted. This is a good way to reflect not only about teaching adults but also in teaching students. If you have taught for several days in a row and have not used any teaching method except lecture, it's time to think about how to reach the students who are not as linguistic or logical so that their learning is strengthened. (See the appendices for a description of community circle, suggested journal prompts, and other MI activities to use in various types of meetings and classes.)

The Myers-Briggs model of temperament is based on four preferences. First, where, primarily, do you direct your energy (introversion or extroversion)? Second, how do you prefer to process information (through physical sensation or intuition)? Third, how do you make decisions (based more on truth or emotions)? How do you organize your life (more by judgment or perception)?

Just as we all possess multiple forms of intelligence, we also all possess the elements in each pair of Myers-Briggs preferences; they are not mutually exclusive. However, we more strongly prefer one side to the other in each domain. For example, I am highly extroverted. This does not mean I do not value my alone time—time to nap, think, read, and write. After a long weekend full of guests to entertain or events to attend, I usually retreat into myself for a couple of days to balance my introvert (I) with my extrovert (E), who has severely overdone it. Likewise, I prefer being around people most of the time. That's why teaching is a terrific occupation for me. I love being in a classroom full of students or working with groups of educators. Education provides a good fit. When I have to sit at my desk, slaving over a report on the computer, I get drained easily because I derive energy from being with others. My husband, on the other hand, is more introverted. If we go to a cocktail party, wedding reception, cookout, or other event with lots of people to talk to, I grow more energetic as the night wears on. I could literally stay out until dawn. He, however, finds a couple of people to converse with at length and is ready to go home when the party is over, even if people are heading out to another fun setting. If I go home with him, I immediately wind down, as I have lost my source of energy—other people. He is exhausted for a different reason—from being in a crowd all evening. We probably keep each other in check quite well. If you are a staff developer, it pays great dividends to realize who your introverts and extroverts are early in the game. You can provide experiences that energize them both at different points in your sessions with them.

The second domain consists of sensation (S) and intuition (N)—the physical versus the mental, if you will. People high in the domain of physical sensation are interested in tangible reality and have an eye for detail. They focus on the present and actual. It's very important when working with these sensors that you embrace the current reality while also trying to get them to see possibilities they may not otherwise see. Intuitors, in contrast, focus on the future rather than the present moment. In working with them, honor their dreams of the future, but take time to show them what is real right now. Sensors may sometimes become too grounded in reality and seem unemotional; intuitors may sometimes seem dreamy, impractical, and unrealistic. It's important to notice patterns of interaction among your inservice participants and to keep pulling both groups back toward the middle. You do not want sensors and intuitors to polarize and square off against each other. Your goal is to help them find common ground, blending current reality with imagined possibilities.

The third domain deals with logic versus emotion. Thinkers (T) make decisions based on objectivity and logic, whereas feelers (F) make decisions based more on personal values, empathy, and compassion. While thinkers love statistics and research, feelers prefer personal anecdotes from others who have implemented what you are discussing. Thinkers are often criticized for being cold or unemotional; feelers are often the ones who withdraw or become visibly emotional if the thinkers in the crowd dominate. My score in thinking is at the top of the scale and my score in feeling is close to zero. Does this mean I am heartless and uncaring? Of course not. It does mean I can easily be *perceived* as such. This is important self-knowledge, because I must guard against alienating the feelers in any crowd I work with. I must also take special precaution in working with supervisors who are more feeling than thinking; I must show that I care first as opposed to showing how much I know first. For me, debating ideas and quoting research sources comes naturally, and I can become quite animated when trying to make a point. I can engage in hearty debate with you and be out to dinner with you one hour later, laughing and joking. The debate, even when contentious, means nothing to me personally. Debate does not affect my personal opinion of you one iota; my love of theory, ideas, and intellectual conversation is totally disconnected from our personal relationship. A feeler may be worried that I dislike him personally or that I am angry about something, when indeed, I am not. In professional development situations, you must help thinkers and feelers learn how not to trample on each other. They complement each other quite nicely, but they must sometimes work to get along, and as a facilitator, you must lead these efforts. Set a tone of respectful discourse and allow for thinkers and feelers to have starring roles at different points in your session.

People high in judgment (J), in the fourth domain of the profile, prefer living in a very structured way. Many teachers are high in judgment and thrive upon the schedules, rules, and set procedures of school. People high in perception (P) prefer more flexibility, discovering life as they go along. These are the teachers who always forget it's their class's turn to use the computer lab and whose lesson plans may vary widely from day to day, depending on what neat idea has just struck them. They hate making quarterly long-range plans and become frustrated with inflexible schedules; they perhaps feel most constrained by the current emphasis on standardized curricula and testing. Judgers often appear organized to the nth degree while perceivers appear so spontaneous that they are sometimes criticized for procrastinating or being too impulsive. Again, the two preferences of judging and perceiving complement each other well, but can create friction in group settings if the leader does not provide stimuli for those of both preferences. For example, an organized agenda given up front is necessary to set the judgers' minds at ease, while some sort of discovery-learning or open-ended task is necessary to cater more to the needs of the perceivers. Judgers like to hold to time limits and sometimes resent long breaks. You can help them deal better with breaks by having some sort of task to complete (even if it's just a "thinking" task). You can help perceivers stay focused by having verbal "check-ins" or short, written tasks interspersed throughout the day. Both groups usually enjoy leaving early, so always overestimate your agenda by fifteen minutes. This is sure to please everyone.

My Myers-Briggs type varies from ESTJ to ENTJ depending on my current work and family situation and has changed like this for the past decade. What this teaches me is that I am fairly balanced in sensation and intuition, but at times one dominates. I am highly thinking and judging without fail. Therefore I must guard against perfectionism and "black/white" thinking. I have to keep my mind open to new possibilities and not get so mired in reality that I fail to be innovative. My extroversion and introversion have been moving closer together as I grow older. Perhaps this is a result of having been so involved in working with students and teachers over the years; I'm finding it necessary to delve into myself more and have found introspection to be a source of energy rather than a source of fatigue.

If you are a staff development facilitator, you must be keenly aware of your own preferences, because you will have to overcome them at times. You will also need to learn to be a quick study to identify the preferences of the people with whom you are working. One critical point: don't take anything personally. People are who they are, and in most cases, they are not intentionally trying to sabotage you or ruin your workshop. They are simply being their own marvelous, multifaceted selves. This diversity is what sometimes makes the work of professional development hard, but it is also what makes it continuously interesting. Just as in K-12 teaching, there is hardly a dull moment in teaching adults!

As you may have guessed by now, I'm a proponent of using activities with teachers to help them uncover or review their own preferences. David Keirsey's book *Please Understand Me II: Temperament, Character, and Intelligence* contains the Keirsey Temperament Sorter, a respected, widely used questionnaire that is very useful in determining personality type. The full Myers-Briggs survey can be administered by licensed practitioners in your area and is a worthwhile endeavor for any faculty, especially at the beginning of a new school year. Thomas Armstrong's book *Seven Kinds of Smart* has a useful self-quiz on MI. His book *Multiple Intelligences in the Classroom* contains the same quiz and also offers dozens of ideas about incorporating MI in your plans for instruction. Both Gardner and Armstrong are cited frequently on the Internet; just search using "multiple intelligences" as the search term and you'll find abundant resources. There are many instruments available and many sources of information on the Internet, some being far superior to others. Refer to the recommended resources in this book and start exploring the various resources about intellect, temperament, and personality.

Once the teachers with whom you are working know themselves a little better, how do they become students again? An elementary teacher could choose part of the required curriculum to explore in depth in a summer graduate course; for example, he could take a course in state history, painting with watercolors, or beginning photography if he has an interest in any of these topics on either a personal or professional level. Unless they are the truest of stay-at-homes or are suffering from extreme primary ignorance, teachers usually connect their own personal explorations with the curriculum being taught. A high school math teacher could enroll in a calculus refresher course. Students look to the teacher to be the best mathematician in the room, so she should certainly stay abreast of mathematics, right? Teachers of all subjects and grade levels are eligible to take summer seminars offered by the National Endowment for the Humanities (NEH) or the National Writing Project (NWP), among many other grant-funded opportunities. If you are a teacher who wants to take it upon yourself to reenergize or refocus your love of learning, you owe it to yourself to truly be a student again. If you are an administrator, commit to encouraging teachers in both material and emotional ways to pursue advanced study. Also consider becoming a student yourself to model the lifelong learning you expect of employees and espouse as a goal for students.

EXEMPLARY STAFF DEVELOPMENT: THE NATIONAL WRITING PROJECT

The NWP is a model of teachers learning as students would. This program is so effective that Ann Lieberman (2000) has called it the best staff development program in the United States.

A core belief of the NWP is that the best teachers of writing are writers themselves. Therefore teachers of writing must write, and not just the routine kinds of writing that teachers often do (memos, reports, handouts, newsletters, lesson plans, discipline referrals, etc.). The NWP summer institute requires teachers to write about self-chosen topics and to share their writing publicly with the group. Some NWP fellows also publish for larger audiences—many for the first time—in professional journals, local newspapers, on websites, and in other ways. The summer institute also requires each teacher to make a formal presentation of a successful teaching practice; for many teachers, this is their first time presenting to peers. Just as classroom teachers expect students to read, write, and present their findings, so do NWP instructors. The summer institute is a very accurate simulation of a "real" K-12 or undergraduate classroom.

Having been an NWP instructor for four summers, I can cite numerous examples of teachers who became passionate students of both reading and writing again. Susan O'Leary, an elementary teacher, is one who said it exceptionally well. She said upon the completion of the CAWP summer institute, "I was never one to write just for the sake of writing, but after attending the institute . . . I find myself frequently looking for a scrap of anything to jot down my thoughts or feelings and then place them in my journal." Susan has definitely internalized the concept of writing for her own purposes, and in the two years since, has shared her enthusiasm with her fourth grade students.

During each of the summers of teaching in the month-long institute, my coteachers and I used a daily writing/art workshop time in addition to a daily silent reading time. We encouraged teachers to write about topics they cared about, prompted by powerful read-alouds, interesting models of good writing, and our own drafts in progress. We strived to demonstrate the connectedness of reading and writing by encouraging them to read self-chosen texts and by doing daily "book talks" high-lighting some of our favorite books. We incorporated art in response to reading and as a stimulus for writing. Daily "art tips" were a non-threatening way to encourage participants to use various media and enjoy playing with their own thinking about literacy and teaching. There are always those people who are more comfortable with reading over writing, or vice versa. Some teachers took readily to writing, sketching, and sharing stories. Others were very apprehensive at first and joined in later. Likewise, some teachers thought periods of silent sustained reading (SSR) were frivolous or unproductive at first, while others could hardly contain their excitement and hauled in piles of books with each successive day.

One 1998 participant said this about SSR: "At first I did not like the reading time. But soon I couldn't wait . . . because I discovered a book that I couldn't stop reading. . . . I finished the book in a day. I started it here [in class] and finished it at home." Another participant that same year said of SSR: "It allows me to . . . step outside of myself and become that other person. . . . It also sparks interesting discussions. I found that in the evening I would read instead of doing other things." Jan Vescovi, also in the 1998 group and a recent college graduate at the time, demonstrates her enthusiasm in this exit slip:

> SSR gave me so much time to read books that I had not had time to read. This made me use every spare minute I had to read: five minutes before I clocked in at work, during my lunch break, and in my car in traffic. . . . I have read seven books including two professional ones. I am so proud of myself for having done this while taking this class and working. I will apply this to my classroom in the fall!

Using art to respond to reading, as impetus for writing, and as a thinking–learning strategy in its own right has received rave reviews for four years, too, even from skeptics (like I was at first). Here are some teachers' comments from the summer of 2000:

"[The] schedule worked better today. . . . What a beautiful lunch. I loved the art lesson!"

"I feel better about writing poetry. Great ideas for getting started. I also enjoy looking at a picture and writing about what I see. . . . It would be interesting to have several people write about the same picture and read several points of view."

"Thank you for the rubrics. . . . Loved the art lessons today. . . . I am amazed at the creativity and energy in this class."

The combination of art and writing even carried over into the daily exit slips teachers wrote. One teacher started embellishing almost all her written feedback with art of some sort. Because we instructors asked the students to write brief daily reflections called exit slips, we were able to immediately capitalize on the teachers' learning and adjust our daily instruction to best suit the needs of our students. We facilitated frequent informal and formal discussions of applying our own "learning about learning" to our classrooms. As Lieberman (2002) has noted, the NWP summer course helps teachers "form a philosophy of teaching" and "think about problems as possibilities for change." Each teacher brings a wealth of experience and practical knowledge to the institute, and conversations are orchestrated to make the most of this expertise.

Several components of the NWP model may be applied to any staff development situation. Among these are social practices (as Lieberman calls them), experiencing the content as a learner and not necessarily an expert, respecting teachers as leaders who can teach their peers, and grounding theory in practice by using current professional literature in the context of rich discussions of classroom realities.

Lieberman notes that the social practices of the NWP are important and serve to build community. In the Coastal Area Writing Project, we build many of our rituals around eating together. Every morning there is fresh coffee and an assortment of breads, sweets, and fruits. The instructors always bring food the first day, but by the third, all we need to do is supply coffee. Everyone starts to pitch in and care for one another by bringing a contribution. One year, we had what we called the "lunch bunch" each day. Teachers were grouped into fours and told to bring a "themed" lunch. The instructors began by doing an American Independence Day theme, complete with red, white, and blue foods and sparklers to light in celebration. With each passing day, lunchtime became more creative and bountiful.

The instructors set a tone of comfort and ownership of the classroom space from day one as well. We usually decorate each table with a couple of fresh flowers or other greenery from the natural world, some nice trinkets that might inspire writing, supplies like scissors and colored pencils, and perhaps some art postcards or other intriguing visuals. As the institute progresses, people bring their own items to add to the mix. A feeling of home pervades, and each table group of three to five people becomes like a family.

Another special social practice is our authors' celebration. This event occurs near the end of the summer institute and features each participant reading aloud a piece of writing that she has developed during the course. Many teachers are so changed by this process of reading aloud and receiving positive feedback that they incorporate similar celebrations into their instruction with overwhelmingly positive results. History teacher Frank Clark referred to the authors' celebration in a journal entry written months later at a continuity meeting: "I very much appreciated the celebration of my fellow students' writing. These celebrations must be passed on to my students. The encouragement and sharing of peers is vital in a democracy. I will continue to reflect on my experiences and encourage my students to develop the same 'esprit de corps.' Learning is a lifelong process, and I hope to inspire that idea [in] my students!"

From day one, participants in the summer institute are writers. They write in response to topics and invitations issued by the instructors. Later comes working with peers to revise, edit, and publish. For many, even though they assign writing to their students, this is the first time in a number of years that they have taken their own work through the entire writing process and explored a writer's craft while they are truly crafting writing themselves.

Lieberman has said that leadership in the Writing Project "becomes something different" (2002). All staff development facilitators could benefit from remembering something the Writing Project firmly believes: everyone in the learning community has expertise and is a potential leader. Everyone is a potential teacher of fellow teachers.

Practice is as valid as theory. All Writing Project participants do a full-length, conference-quality presentation during the summer institute; at many sites, teachers do more than one. I have used a combination of two presentations successfully: one, a fifteen-minute strategy sharing session; and two, a one-hour, conference-type, formal presentation. The short presentation comes during the first week of the course and is planned prior to the summer. The longer presentation is given during the last few days of the course. The instructors or past WP fellows first model this kind of presentation and then allow participants to use peer response groups to plan their own. The class also creates a rubric together based on the modeled presentations. The rubric becomes the guideline for presentation development.

Talking about teaching and talking about professional literature are important components of the NWP, too, and are central to all good staff development. Writing Project fellows always read at least one professional book together as the core of the class; often we have read and discussed two. Conversations based on topics that arise from the books take place during structured times and, of course, informally as participants work together in their table groups, enter each morning, or return from the lunch break. During one summer, teachers kept saying things like, "When school starts, I'm gonna have SSR" and "I'm gonna do peer response groups." As a result, I taped poster paper on the wall and labeled it "I'm gonna." Daily, as someone thought of something he or she wanted to change in the new school year and said, "I'm gonna," we wrote the promise on the poster paper. This made for visual reinforcement of the learning and served as a catalyst for discussion during transition times in class.

STORIES: TEACHERS AS LEARNERS

The NWP believes that instructors must experience the assignments they are using with the institute participants, so I have four journals packed with my own summer institute writing, among other, more personal journals I have kept. Allow me to share from my own writing before I highlight the writing of teachers with whom I've worked.

The first reflection was written in response to the prompt, "When I am thinking at my best. . . ." The goal here is for teachers to think about their own learning processes, which are later discussed and framed in terms of theory (like constructivism) and direct application to the classroom.

> When I am thinking at my best, I'm like a fire. I crackle and burn and consume all there is in my path. I just eat it up, and it fuels me. I can't get enough knowledge when I'm deeply engaged in learning something. For example, when I was doing my dissertation research, I would be so swept up in it for hours on end—books and papers scattered all around, and I would just dive in—they would ignite me! I sought more and more—kept looking, kept engulfing everything in my path. . . . Fire symbolizes passion, and I have a real passion for learning.

During another summer institute, I responded to the prompt "My mind is like. . . ." in this entry:

> Sometimes my mind is like a rubber band—pulled taut, almost ready to snap. At other times, my mind is fluid—leisurely floating from this idea to that one, drifting along like a river on a cloudless, windless day. Some days, my mind darts and flits like a rabbit in the woods—pausing here and there to concentrate or to nibble, then scurrying away when threat arrives. Other days, my mind lies still, basking in the sunlight like a just-fed cat, lingering in naps and dreams. My mind is often simultaneously full and empty, nervous and serene, confident and frightened, disinterested and engaged. Ah, you see, my mind can't make up its mind!

Asking teachers to think about metaphors for their minds or their intelligence is a rich activity that leads to greater insight about one's learning. Discussions arise about constructivist theory, multiple intelligences, emotional intelligence, learning disabilities, and many other pedagogical topics. The writing that results may also be used with students to have them explore the same issues. Here is Frank Clark's response to the "thinking at my best" prompt: "I equate that with the printing press as it spits out a non-stop stream of work. . . . My results are all genuine copies. . . . I picture the press to be in black and white, not a myriad of colors. My mind is also going at full speed at this prolific time."

Frank's metaphor is mechanical, fast, and precise. Think about how this metaphor could apply to his teaching. Does he expect students to have "printing press" minds, too? How does he allow for "rabbit" minds like the one I wrote about—the mind that stops, considers, wanders, nibbles, and plays? These are important questions for a teacher to consider when assessing his own practice, and these questions formed a basis of discussion between Frank and me.

Frank also responded to the prompt "My mind is like. . . ." in art and writing. His short, written response was, "The brain is like an inlet. Fresh water and thoughts are vital." He accompanied it with a watercolor drawing. During the entire summer institute, Frank's reflective writing contained many natural images—images of the beach, ocean, trees, breezes, etc. However, it is not clear from his journal entries how he connected this obvious pull toward nature with his teaching of social studies. What he did connect was his newfound pleasure in writing.

Another prompt we used was, "What does it mean to be creative?" Because we were using Michael Gelb's book *How to Think Like Leonardo da Vinci* as a core text, we often discussed the concepts of intelligence, creativity, and art. Here is Frank's reflection about being creative:

> There are different ways of being creative. Some of us feel creative time is time not at work, where we stop a part of life . . . to recreate a peaceful or rejuvenated state. . . . The more desirable definition would be to be creative in all aspects of life . . . to be eloquent, yet forceful, in the way we face each and every situation. . . . If we actively look at each situation as one to be enjoyable and a learning, God-given experience, how can we fail?

Frank's views on creativity are worthy of exploring with his high school students. Knowing that he implemented journal writing in his social studies classroom as a result of taking the Writing Project, I'm sure discussions of creativity abound.

One time, after reading aloud a chapter from Stephen King's book *On Writing*, we asked the teachers to describe their ideal writing space—one that would foster experimentation and positive feelings about writing. This is Frank's response:

My ideal writing space would certainly be out of doors. There would be a cool breeze engulfing me . . . the lapping of waves, the running of the river, or the sound of leaves rustling. . . . I would be alone, but not lonely, as the cues of life would teem all around me. . . . There would be space for my thoughts and experiences to join with those around me. My senses would all be enhanced to "join in" and participate.

Frank definitely shows some traits of the person high in sensation on the Myers-Briggs scale. This journal entry became an impetus for him to explore how he assigned writing in his classes: Were students forced to sit in desks? Did they have to remain quiet? What to do with those who enjoy movement, sound, or nature? In the following school year, he e-mailed me periodically to keep me updated on how his teaching had changed, and the biggest area of change was in how he planned for, assigned, and evaluated writing. He also took a graduate course I taught, so we got to continue exploring the issues he uncovered in the summer and tackle new issues as well.

In the summer institute, we often ask teachers to write specifically about themselves as writers, to focus on their own writing process, and to ponder what they want to write about. On the first day of class in 2001, Frank was showing apprehension but willingness in this entry:

The start of a week, a class, a thought. Build on this foundation. Isn't it great to have 'fresh' starts? . . . I need to pool my thoughts, organize creativity? Bottle it? How do you polish a piece of writing? Does it shine afterwards, glow, or smell of lemon? I am grateful to have this course to give me the structure to . . . enhance my thoughts. Random is good, but my mind always seeks order. . . . Where are my perceptions coming from? Do I control them, or do they control me? . . . Can a person shed old, tired thoughts like a snake sheds skin? I dream of spiritual renewal. . . . Do I dare get my hopes up? . . . Can I learn what I hope to teach others?

What phenomenal questions Frank asks himself here. He discusses his goals for learning and for life while also contemplating the intricacies of his thinking/writing process.

Gretchen Meier, an NWP fellow in 2000, also wrote of herself as a writer:

There is sort of a dichotomy about being an English teacher. You are expected to have this love of writing, and I can't say that I do. What I am discovering is that I have a desire. Not for writing so much to share but for me. . . . I realize the easy road is to just sit back and turn on the TV . . . and the difficult road would be to explore me. . . . What I can't determine is if I feel a huge desire or a huge pressure to "create." I want to be silly, but I don't want to look back with disdain and think, "how silly." I want to feel enlightened but not falsely. I want to be that creative person, but again, do I want it for me or for appearance's sake? I'm trying to locate if there is an empty spot. Does it really exist or do I say it exists? Sometimes when I think things and then I write them down, they seem to lose their validation. Is that in my head . . . or is it that I almost subconsciously seem scared of myself?

Gretchen speaks eloquently about the peer pressure that teachers often feel. She also shows an openness to learning, to experimentation. She is, in this entry, starting to explore herself as a learner, teacher, and writer, in a three-pronged but unified approach. She did go on to complete the Writing Project successfully and even took two additional graduate courses cosponsored by the Writing Project and its local university affiliate. Gretchen became a writer of both personal and professional pieces as well as a skilled presenter and mentor to other teachers.

One technique taught in the summer institute is the use of a "brain drain" time in which everyone writes to get worrisome thoughts out of their minds. Here is one of Gretchen's brain drain writings:

It is time to drain my brain. Drain it of what, I ask? If I turn on the [spigot] will it stop? My brain cannot really drain. It feels stopped up. Maybe there is too much hair in the trap. Joy, oh joy! Joy! It was quiet. Historical diaries, witches, and ponds, cops and crimes, reading buddies. The yearbook is *almost* late! I don't feel like I am living any questions because I'm bobbing in the water, not just floating along but bobbing, bobbing, bobbing, feeling like I'm doing a hell of a job but starting to question the relevance. Kids talking about raping and stabbing and stealing and I want them to enjoy *The Witch of Blackbird Pond?* I can relate it to them but their minds are so cluttered with other things. . . . I'm becoming one of them!

This brain drain clearly shows how teachers' teaching lives seep into all that they do. Gretchen starts writing about the brain drain technique itself and her own writing process but ends up discussing teaching, the literature she teaches, and how her mind works in ways similar to the minds of her students. Because Gretchen took another graduate course with me the semester after this entry was written, I know that she changed how she used literature in her classroom. Perhaps this entry was a precursor to that change. It's obvious that she was already thinking about how to make reading more relevant and engaging for her students and that she was experiencing some frustration with her own instruction. These "probletunities" turned into a classroom inquiry and led her to new ways of teaching.

Cathy Green took a writing prompt based on the poem "The Sacred" by Stephen Dunning and used it to write about her deepest values and beliefs:

> My sacred place is deep within my mind. It is my armor from the bad. It is a place I don't quite understand but am delighted by.
>
> When I need to "adjust my sails," I go to my sacred place for comfort and wellness. It is there [that] I have all the tools needed to lift up my chin, look straight forward, and start over.
>
> My sacred place allows me to be sane and feel good about myself no matter what craziness I am caught up in. It is a place free from lurking demons. It is my good voice deep inside my soul.
>
> My sacred place allows me optimism. It allows me sanity. It is my clock, my path . . . my joy.

Fedrick Cohens writes of his sacred place in a much more concrete way:

> One place that I can mention as being special or sacred is my own bedroom. Countless hours are spent there relaxing, working, listening, thinking, or writing. Those four walls . . . serve a purpose in my life. They provide shelter in rough times and solitude at other times. It's a haven of sorts. Whatever I do, wherever I go, and with whom I'm going is usually decided in my room. My bedroom, a sacred place with a voice. A voice that gives me directions and advice.

Both Cathy and Fedrick's entries equate the sacred place with a voice guiding them. This voice seems to be the inner self that helps make decisions about not only personal matters but work-related matters as well. This powerful prompt allows for teachers to explore their deepest held beliefs, and often, information about teaching shines through as well. Teachers like Cathy and Fedrick are most likely to stay focused even in times of great stress at work, as long as they remember to go back to that inner voice they trust. (See appendix B for suggested journal prompts.)

In the Writing Project and in every graduate course I teach, at some point I ask students what helped support them as learners. Perhaps it is appropriate to close this chapter with Al Wendler's brainstormed list of words on this topic. His list is a good one to keep in the back of one's mind when planning any kind of staff development: no put-downs, immersion, "who" instead of "what," sharing, presentations, feeling worthwhile, feedback on everything, willingness, comfortable, congenial, time together, teachers doing the work along with students, choice, time, no pressure, validation, trust, ambiance, modeling, community, inspiration, humor, freedom, passion for learning, knowledgeable teachers, flexibility, art, fun, informative, projects, clear purposes, collaboration, books, emotional.

RESPONSE QUESTIONS FOR CHAPTER 3

1. When your mind is working at its best, to what could you compare it? What does this comparison show you about your learning?
2. When you are struggling with learning something, to what could you compare your mind? How does the struggle make you feel? How can you apply this understanding to students who struggle with learning new material?
3. When planning the next presentation you will give or the next class you will teach, how can you apply some of the words listed at the end of the chapter? For example, how will you *immerse* the learners in the learning? How will you provide *feedback*? How will *fun* and *humor* play a role?

CHAPTER 4

Inside-Out as a Teacher

"The challenge of teaching is to decide who you want to be as a teacher, what you care about and what you value, and how you will conduct yourself in classrooms with students."

—William Ayers in *To Teach: The Journey of a Teacher*

"Education . . . calls for some spirited and creative innovations both in the substance and the purpose of current pedagogy. . . . Only when we have worked purposefully and long on a problem that interests us, and in hope and in despair wrestled with it in silence and alone relying on our own unshaken will—only then have we achieved education."

—Ann Sullivan Macy

Teachers must know themselves as learners, but this self-knowledge is not separate from knowing themselves as teachers. The processes are intertwined and complementary. There are lapses of time in which teachers do not experience learning as much from a student or "novice" stance as from a professional or "expert" one, but this does not mean that vocational learning is not taking place. The "undivided self" Parker Palmer (1997) speaks of is evident as teachers connect their teaching selves with their learning selves in professional development situations. The trick for the astute staff developer is to get the teacher to elucidate her professional learning, bring forth the educational theory embedded within, and teach more strategically as a result. The connection is the critical juncture for the staff developer and must be reinforced through professional reading and ongoing collegial dialogue.

We educators, like all humans, are learning all the time we are living, but we may grow comfortable enough with our expertise that we feel we know it all about teaching. This kind of complacency, even if momentary, is sinister. It is a manifestation of primary ignorance or the beginning of apathy or arrogance. To combat the serious consequences of complacency, educators must engage in inside-out staff development experiences focused directly upon the teaching act.

"GROWING" TEACHERS: TOOLS THAT WORK

Several inside-out processes work with all teachers. Because these methods work so well and are relatively inexpensive, they are high-yield in terms of cost versus benefits. This section will focus on these high-yield tools, and further illustration will follow in the "stories" section.

Methods discussed include the following: using teaching journals, conducting classroom inquiry/research projects, observing teachers (including various forms of notetaking and follow-up conversation), reading professional materials, and attending professional conferences (with specific follow-up at the job site).

Keeping a teaching journal is the one method I endorse above all others. The second method I recommend is the personalized classroom inquiry project, which is also almost fail-proof and results in reflection as well as action. Both of these self-directed, immediately relevant processes work well in all phases of a teacher's career, with teachers of all grade levels and subject areas, and in any size or type of school.

I've used two types of observations with success. One is the observation followed by written feedback and coaching, which is most useful for experienced teachers who are performing satisfactorily or better. The other type differs slightly. It involved transcription and is usually done in a series, with focused, follow-up conversation. Observations open the classroom and the teaching act up to examination, much like a teaching hospital makes actual medical practice more public and more collegial. We must openly scrutinize our own practice plus the practice of peers and subordinates in order to better understand teaching and to improve it.

Two other methods with real impact are reading professional books (whether done individually or in groups) and attending professional conferences (again, individually or in groups). With substantial conversation, observation, and other types of follow-up, these two methods enhance and extend the more hands-on, personalized methods of journal writing, individualized inquiry, and one-to-one coaching.

High-Yield Process #1: Teaching Journals

Since 1998, I've used teaching journals successfully in several diverse groups and have seen remarkable change connected to their use. The groups include twenty-seven K–12 teachers piloting district curriculum standards (1994–1995), the entire academic faculty of a Jewish day school (1998–2002), participants in the Coastal Area Writing Project (1998–2001), three groups of secondary teachers enrolled in graduate-level education courses (2000–2003), and seven teachers comprising the language arts department of a rural, high-poverty, low-performing school (2002–2003). Most of the examples I cite in this chapter are the more recent ones (to which I have better access), but they parallel numerous examples from my own teaching journals, from the journals of other teachers with whom I've worked, and from published professional literature.

Journals take various forms and range from totally private and personalized to totally public with inflexible parameters. The continuum in figure 4.1 depicts the various forms. I prefer to use types to the left of center with teachers, as I feel the more flexible the journal is, the more powerful it becomes for its owner. To me, the journal is a tool for self-reflection and growth, not a gauge of effectiveness. For more public accountability purposes, like National Board certification or local professional development documentation, the types to the right of center may be more appropriate.

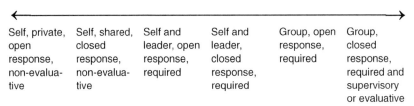

Figure 4.1. *Types of teaching journals.*

I don't mean to oversimplify journals or make them sound silly, but to me, keeping a teaching journal is like buying a dress for a very special occasion. First, you think about what kind of dress you're looking for, what will make the right impression, and what will be comfortable but stylish. When you enter the store, you describe this vision to the salesperson. You verbalize your thinking. Then, you try on selected dresses and check the fit. You ask yourself, does it work? How will others respond? Will they think I look glamorous, sexy, businesslike, too short, too heavy, too young, too old, or what? Then you do the actual work of checking the fit. You may walk out to the three-way mirrors, sit, stand, bend over, twirl. Does it seem to match the situation you intend it for? Is it just the right thing for that graduation, wedding, ball, retirement dinner, or memorial service, since there is a specific protocol for each? (It may even cross your mind to challenge the protocol—to wear white to a wedding or a bright color to a funeral, just because it looks good or perhaps even to get a certain reaction.) Next, you check out the reactions of an audience—your friends or family, probably. You may ask, would you wear this if you were I? What will everyone think of this? Have you been to something like this occasion before? What did you wear? Finally, you've made your final selection and attend the event. The next step is either positive or negative reaction to the event, and perhaps even to your choice of clothing. "It was so tight, I could hardly enjoy the wonderful buffet," you tell your pals. Or you admit your feet hurt in that gorgeous pair of perfectly matching slingbacks. The other possibility is, of course, that the dress worked perfectly, netting you comfort, beauty, and compliments. In this case, your after-event talk is more celebratory.

An uncomplicated comparison, perhaps, but similar to the use of teaching journals. Writing in a journal is often like experimenting with one's wardrobe, although it is far more than surface-level. Teachers do all of the following in their teaching journals:

- describe metacognitive processes, thinking not only about their own thinking but also thinking about their teaching;
- "try on" strategies, lessons, and ideas about both theory and practice;
- align theory with practice and vice versa;

- respond to colleagues in several ways (first, to the conversations/ dialogue of peers in classes or inservices; to the presentations of peers, who may be of equal status or who may be professional consultants; and lastly, to distant peers or mentors who have published their work);
- vent frustrations;
- find affirmation and celebrate successes.

Both journals and classroom inquiry projects take what is within the teacher's mind in combination with his outward actions, using both as a basis for reflection and growth. Both can be merged with periodic observations by a chosen colleague, a site-based mentor or coach, or a supervisor, not only to assist the teacher in continuous staff development but also to form *portions* of a fuller, fairer teacher evaluation process. Although my goal is not to recommend journals, inquiry projects, and observations as methods of evaluation, there is potential for all of these components to be incorporated into a well-rounded system of teacher evaluation. I do believe, however, that *evidence of participation* in reflective activities like the ones described in this chapter could be a staff development requirement that would be *part (and only part)* of humane, multidimensional teacher evaluation.

High-Yield Process #2: Classroom Research

The five teachers of academic subjects at the Chabad Academy in Myrtle Beach, South Carolina, conducted focused classroom research in the 1998–1999 school year. Each teacher, her questions, and possible sources of data are shown in appendix C. Throughout the year, we discussed and refined the questions, determined appropriate teaching strategies, and collected and analyzed data. In extensive interviews with two of the teachers at the end of the year, they felt overwhelmingly positive about the inquiry/collaboration process (Peery 2000).

Other, more informal classroom research was conducted by eight graduate students in a class I taught in 2003. Several teachers wanted to combine fun, creative, effective reading activities with preparation for standardized testing. One teacher wanted to make a particularly uninteresting novel that she was required to teach more interesting through drama, hands-on activities, and use of technology. Another gave her students a reading comprehension test, tracked their progress through the semester as she used research-based teaching methods, and then tested students again at the end. They showed significant reading growth.

How does one begin a cycle of inquiry at a school site? Department or grade-level chairpersons could serve as liaisons as a whole faculty engages in classroom research. Inquiry questions do not have to involve sophisticated statistical analysis (although they certainly may). Anecdotal notes, student work samples, and student interviews all reveal information about teaching and learning.

One of the best ways to begin an inquiry is to read a shared professional text or follow-up from a dynamic presenter. Reading professional literature and attending thought-provoking presentations should naturally cause "what if?" questions to arise in teachers' minds, and these "what ifs" can be turned into inquiry studies. (See appendix D for more information about beginning inquiry at your school.)

High-Yield Process #3: Observations with Feedback

Observations, whether by self, peer, or supervisor, are a critical component of professional growth. Teaching is one of the few professions in which much of the work takes place behind a closed door with no other adult in the room. I myself have gone an entire school year with the principal coming in to watch me teach once for about twenty minutes, and colleagues coming in only when they needed to ask a question, borrow supplies, or see a student—never to thoughtfully observe. While this phenomenon of concealment of practice is slowly changing, open scrutiny in education has not caught up with that of medical, legal, and other fields. Opening the classroom doors, having observers talk with teacher and students, and allowing observers to record and respond to instruction (not just classroom management) are nonnegotiable in inside-out professional development.

The Basic Transcription Process

The transcription process I used for several years is outlined below. Examples of transcripts and discussion of the coaching that went along with transcription is more fully described in the "stories" section later in this chapter.

1. Be a careful observer. Write down all you see and hear for a period of at least twenty minutes or one complete class activity. Be sure to note facial expressions, body language, and actual words spoken by both teacher and students. Note the time in the margins of your notes periodically.
2. Provide the transcript to the teacher within twenty-four hours. Type it after the observation if it's not legible. If the handwriting is legible or it's too time-consuming to type your notes, provide the teacher with a photocopy.
3. Invite the teacher to confer with you as follow-up, or depending upon your level of concern, insist on it. Exemplary teachers should be invited. Satisfactory teachers should be scheduled for an appointment. Teachers with severe problems—those bordering on incompetence—must be pursued and addressed immediately.
4. In the conference, ask the teacher, "What did you see in the transcript? What is worthy of discussion here?" If possible, let the teacher lead the discussion. This is where the real learning takes place. If you have serious concerns, however, be more direct and more authoritarian as the situation warrants.
5. Plan for ongoing follow-up.

For a master teacher or one you have little concern about, simply say that you'll be back soon for another visit. Make a point to do this in the following few weeks, and confer afterward if the teacher wants to. Your observation should be of similar length as the first one and ideally would be of a different group of students or different time of day. Don't neglect these "star" teachers; they need feedback in order to grow, and sometimes we forget about them as we concentrate on those who seem to need more help.

For a teacher you have some concerns about, arrange a longer visit. Allow the teacher to pick the date and time and look for specific improvement in things that you and the teacher have already discussed. Provide positive feedback about the noted improvements.

For a teacher you have serious concerns about, arrange a longer visit, perhaps a whole class period. Agree upon the date and time with the teacher; in this way, you can expect the teacher to feel comfortable and to do a showcase lesson. Confer after the observation and conduct an *unannounced* visit shortly afterward. *The unannounced visit is important to help you document either improvement or ongoing problems.* Continue the cycle of observations and conferences until the problems you noted are under control or you decide to take other action.

In my varied experiences transcribing since 1994, good teachers glean much more from the transcripts than I ever expected, mediocre teachers strive to improve and benefit from the follow-up coaching, and incompetent teachers realize it's time to find an occupation at which they can be more successful.

High-Yield Process #4: Professional Reading

Teachers cannot improve their craft without reading about teaching and reading specialized materials about the content they teach. Teachers who aren't readers frighten me: just what have they been exposed to if they haven't been reading about what other teachers are doing in the classroom? Who wants an English teacher who doesn't read new literature? Who wants a science teacher who is not familiar with recent scientific research?

In one school for which I consulted, the principal went to a summer leadership institute and returned wanting to do a whole-faculty study of two professional books, *Classroom Instruction That Works* and *Learning by Heart*. I suggested that we start with the first, as it contains numerous examples of actual classroom practice and has short, readable chapters. Both texts provided fodder for rich discussion in a series of monthly meetings. (Sample agendas from our book discussion meetings appear in appendix E.)

A long, long time ago, in a school district far, far away, where I once worked, a principal bought each teacher a copy of a cutesy, best-selling, business management-type book and asked them to read it over the summer. This move brought kudos to the principal from the superintendent, but, according to one teacher I talked with, produced very little in the way of changed practice.

There is nothing wrong with asking one's faculty to read a book;

however, the book must become the basis for serious conversation and action. Teachers and principals suffer from overload: we are bombarded with written messages and all sorts of text to read daily. A slim volume of maxims to apply to our daily work will be read much like junk food is eaten—it will be gulped down quickly but will provide little real nutrition. If you want people to be nourished from their professional reading, you must make the dining experience memorable and linger over it.

How about giving teachers a book and saying "use it"? This has happened twice in one school where I worked. Have the books been used? No. And it's too bad, because in both instances, the books would have been excellent resources for teaching writing across the curriculum. If money is being spent in these tightwad times, *there must be follow-up.* Otherwise, teaching remains unchanged and resources gather dust on bookshelves.

High-Yield Process #5: Attending Professional Conferences

Teachers usually return from professional conferences excited about new ideas and resources they have discovered. Denise Stanley shows her exuberance about having attended a statewide literacy conference in this response:

> My reaction to the conference? I thought it was awesome! I attended several sessions that were very beneficial. Of course, I think the three general sessions were super. I could have listened to [author] Lester Laminack all day! [Author] Patricia Polacco was new to me, and I have discovered an excellent source of read-alouds after hearing her. . . . Janet Allen was wonderful. Her enthusiasm alone was worth listening to . . . but the book titles and ideas about teaching were tremendous.

The rest of Denise's response, posted online for her classmates in a graduate course, details the breakout sessions she attended, shows connections she made to her teaching, and offers to share pertinent handouts.

If state or national professional organizations offer conferences in your area, it pays far beyond dollars to send teachers. Granted, if overnight accommodations, meals, and travel are factored in, sending teachers may seem expensive, but still, it's worth it. I have never failed to see teachers return from a high-quality conference with attitudes of openness and excitement. The trick, of course, is to nurture these attitudes and use them as a basis for improving instruction.

STORIES: THE PROCESSES IN ACTION

Journals

Promoting Metacognition

One of the best ways of promoting thinking about your own thinking and thinking about your teaching is to read professional materials and respond in a double-entry journal. There are many formats for double-entry journals, but my favorite is to have participants respond to powerful quotations. The quotes may be assigned prior to the reading, or each reader may select his own significant passages. (My double-entry journal on the professional book *Mind Matters* [Kirby and Kuykendall 1991] appears in figure 4.2.)

Responding to text is somewhat distant and structured. Let's go more deeply into the personal and unstructured. Several times I have asked teachers to write and draw metaphors for their own teaching. One summer, I surprised even myself by comparing the act of teaching to the act of writing a poem. I created a visual with oil pastels and then wrote several drafts of a poem. The final draft appears below and remains untitled.

> With what does the poet work?
> Words, lines, metaphors, rhymes.
> For the teacher: standards, schedules, budding young minds.
> The poet's inspiration—love, music, art, nature, beauty.
> The teacher's—children, learning, a sense of calling and duty.
> The world greets the poet's finished product, standing alone,
>   printed on a page.
> The teacher's art, forever unfinished, greets the world, striving
>   to find its place.

Provocative Quote	My Thoughts
When it comes to thinking and learning and growing, conditions count. (p. 22)	The classroom must induce thinking, not hinder it.
Classroom as "sort of like a womb" (p. 23)	Comfortable, providing sustenance.
We must swear off short-term, highly defined tasks and questions with easy, stock answers. (p. 23)	No vocab quizzes every Friday! No matching section on the test! What are my tests, anyway??? How to be more authentic???
From Peter Elbow: We should see our students as smart and capable. . . . We should look beyond their mistakes or ignorance to the intelligence that lies behind it. (p. 25)	An error still has a thinking pattern behind it. As a teacher, it is my responsibility to try to understand the "smartness" of a student's error.
We don't think that students should be the only ones to take chances. . . . We must push ourselves beyond sure-fire correctness. (p. 26)	I must push myself to question and to experience the reading and writing processes I am asking them to experience.
It is good to rub and polish our brain against that of others. (p. 27)	Collaboration is good for thinking—for both adults and for kids.
As teachers of language, we know first-hand the importance of cultivating collaborative thinking. (p. 29)	Language connects humans. A language class should be filled with the voices of students.
Designing the kinds of tasks we'll be talking about . . . takes us to the edge of our competence; there's so much we don't yet know. (p. 30)	I can never be sure if I'm "getting at" what's important—but taking the time to examine what I'm doing makes me a better teacher.
Just how does practice look in the classroom? . . . It often looks a lot like art. . . . In the first place, thinking, like art, involves making—as in constructing, forming, and composing. . . . It elicits the kind of total engagement for which Bruner borrows from a colleague the coinage *perfink* to encompass perception, feeling, and thinking. To that, we would add doing. (p. 35)	I want to have "perfinking" going on in my classroom all the time—like a studio for learning! Everyone is busy creating, collaborating, and discussing their meaning-making . . .
Students don't mind working hard; they do mind being bored by rote, low-quality tasks that engage neither body nor mind. (p. 36)	This is so true. I can get high-quality work even from very low-level students if I design meaningful, engaging, personally relevant tasks.
People are not recorders of information but makers of meaning. (p. 37)	Lecturing encourages recording. What activities encourage *making meaning*???

Figure 4.2. *Chapter 2 of* Mind Matters—*Teach for Thinking? How?*

In the same workshop, Cathy Green drew an image of a humming-bird and wrote this to accompany it: "When I teach well, I am a hum-mingbird: graceful, busy, going where I need to, when I'm supposed to. Alighting on children, doing my job, and moving on quickly."

As we reexperience subject matter through the eyes of a student, we think like students as we also think like teachers. As part of a graduate education course in teaching reading to secondary students, all partici-pants (including myself) read at least one young adult novel. Many of us end up reading several because we find so many to pique our interest through book talks shared with each other online and in class. In this weekly journal entry, Sharon Cunningham shows the enthusiasm of reading a great book along with the continuous "how do I apply this to my teaching?" thoughts teachers carry around in their heads:

> Response to *Holes*: What an unusual novel! Several of my students saw me reading this during SSR. I received varying responses. The male response was more positive than the female. . . . I'm not really sure why. Maybe the predominantly male character list or the Old West type refer-ences. The "good guy wins" ending would normally turn me off. How-ever, I found it refreshing after reading *The Lovely Bones*. *Holes* was so far removed from reality that it is hard to connect. . . . My student that enjoyed *The Sisterhood of the Traveling Pants* read *Holes* next. She wasn't very enthusiastic. Her apathetic response did give us an opportu-nity to discuss the novel. I think she felt very "smart" to privately ana-lyze a novel with me. Our private discussion did lure a few other students who had read *Holes*. It evolved into a very positive experience. . . . I found a useful lesson plan for *Holes* on the web. It was somewhat con-ventional in its format, but there were elements that could be useful in developing reading strategies.

Sharon the engaged reader is also Sharon the ever-thinking teacher. She has done the following in her journal entry: compared the book to other books read, a skill all good readers employ; analyzed the appeal of the book and noted that it may be related to gender; modeled engaged reading for her students; discussed a teaching strategy (confer-ring with students about reading); demonstrated how she researched using the book in the future by finding a suitable lesson plan; and dem-onstrated deep reflection about her teaching methods. The power of doing ourselves what we ask of students—reading, writing, and reflecting on our own learning—is *phenomenal.* Sharon exhibits this power in this journal entry, which is just one of many she wrote during the semester she spent in an education methods class.

Classmate Ann Twigg responds to the book *Stargirl* by Jerry Spinelli:

> *Stargirl.* My heart hurts. Matt [husband] just came into the bedroom and asked why I was crying. If only I were a little younger, a little bolder . . . I'd change my name to Wildflower, just for a day. I would find my enchanted place and visit at least three times a week. I'd read the fillers in the newspaper and listen more to the gossip when I get my hair cut. I'd learn to play the ukulele and cheer for the other team. . . . Stargirl, where are you? A precious story for any teenager, especially one who feels he/she has to fit the norm and be like everyone else . . . and for one who doesn't. A favorite among many of my young adult novels.

Trying On Strategies

Teachers preplan instruction in their journals. Wanda Freeman had this to say after reading an article about using audiotaped books in language arts classes:

> Could I really read all period with my students? I know they would like it, but could it work? Some already like to read. Some really, really *hate* to read. I wonder what would happen if I chose a book and . . . just kept at it until I finished it. I may just try it. I need to check with Phyllis [media specialist] to see how many books on tape we have and if there are enough tape recorders. I can let them read in class every day, maybe twenty minutes Monday through Thursday and thirty-five minutes on Friday. How would I monitor their comprehension? Response journals, questions about reading, confer with some while others read? I am looking for strategies that will allow me to work guilt-free. . . .

Wanda not only tries on a strategy (listening to books on tape), but she also starts plotting out time increments, planning for collaboration, and designing assessment tasks.

A teacher in a graduate course I taught in 2001 said this in one journal entry:

> Another strategy that I want to use (I think it is a strategy—or maybe an idea) is to have interesting poems on an overhead. Read one aloud every day or use them to introduce ideas for writing. I like how in class we read several in a row like this and then were able to have writing time to write about something, a memory perhaps, that was awakened by a phrase or word in the poem. . . . Of course I will use this routinely in writing workshop. I am currently scouting out some good poems to use. . . . I'll use this with the regular class because there are students here that would really get into this activity. It may be lost on the kids that are always off task, but hey! You never know. Poetry may be the key!

The teacher is deciding to use a technique modeled in the graduate course and is seeing how it may be effective with student-writers because it was effective with her. In looking for poems to use, she is being an active reader while also being a reading teacher. Also in this entry, she is modeling positive attitudes not only about reading but also about learning and teaching.

Olga Toggas wrote about how she would use an activity she read about in a professional book: "The 'seen vs. unseen' activity will take place in my classroom on Friday. I *loved* how she [the author] manipulated this activity. I wanted my students to . . . create an epilogue to *The Pearl*, but naturally, I'd like for it to be one that is feasible. When demonstrated in this manner, maybe my students would get it and be able to be creative and thorough as opposed to outlandish."

Thinking through future lessons as these teachers have done is a valuable activity and helps teachers avoid assigning mundane or nonengaging tasks.

Aligning Theory with Practice

Cathy Green and Fedrick Cohens provide two of the most compelling examples of revised pedagogy in journal entries they created.

In a graduate course offered as a follow-up to the summer Writing Project, Cathy and Fedrick, along with the other participants, started class one evening by responding to a journal prompt that asked them to represent what they had taken back to their teaching from our summer and additional semester together. Cathy juxtaposed the passion and self-direction of Writing Project-type instruction on one side of the paper and, on the reverse, wrote about how her school district's administration seemed to encourage robotic thinking and unquestioning compliance. Fedrick used the image of the ocean to write and draw his ideas.

The text of his writing reads:

> Writing waves. The Coastal Writing Project has been an enlightening experience. I have thoroughly enjoyed myself. It's as if I have recovered from a strong undercurrent and now rest on the waves of writing. I am confident in my writing. I am willing to share it with others, both young and old. My writing practices have improved. I put emphasis on content and meaning. I write more! I teach writing as if it were English or math. Children only know as much as you teach them. I have developed a community of writers. My students love writing and can't wait to do it. Writing, music, and art can be integrating. Using one form promotes the other one.

In this entry, Fedrick touches upon current recommendations about modeling desired behaviors, immersing students in writing, valuing content over form (working on conventions only after fluency has been achieved); and using multiple intelligences research to guide instruction. His practical experiences have helped educational theory take hold and come to life.

Responding to Presentations

Here are some reflection questions to use with any presentation. They may be used as the basis of a journal entry or may be answered on a slip of paper to give to the presenter for feedback purposes.

1. What I enjoyed most about your presentation:
2. What I found most useful:
3. A question or suggestion:
4. Other comments:

Sharon Cunningham responded to Gretchen Meier's videotaped presentation in this way:

What a treat to see Gretchen again—even though it was only by video! I purchased . . . *When Kids Don't Read: What Teachers Can Do* last weekend. I have had time only to peruse the chapters. Gretchen's presentation gave me the opportunity to interactively focus on some key strategies. I was flipping pages like a crazy person trying to locate the strategies and activities Gretchen was discussing. Many of the strategies I have used before. Being relatively new after having taken an eleven-year hiatus, I'm not as fluent . . . as most of you guys. Lately I have found myself overwhelmed with great ideas. I jot notes . . . everywhere. Eventually I will find these ideas. I am becoming better at making lesson plans and going, "Hey, I can use Janet Allen's idea of. . . ." You veterans are much better at this.

The presentation gave Sharon ideas about practice and also led her into studying her new professional book more in depth. Without the "nudge" from Gretchen's presentation, she may have put the book aside for a while and regretted it later, noting strategies she could have employed immediately. Also, in her entry, Sharon demonstrates how she is able to synthesize the many ideas of professional authors into daily planning. Through the required reading and presentations by local practitioners in the graduate course, Sharon became more comfortable with seeking out ideas and integrating them into her repertoire.

In response to a presentation by teacher and consultant Ginger Manning, teacher Rebecca Helms had this to say:

Ginger's presentation was great, too—again, immediately useful! She used the perfect poem to demonstrate how engagement levels change with understanding. We expect our students to get excited about material before we let them discover its meanings and feel the success of understanding. . . . This activity . . . would work even with lower-level readers because they share success with other students . . . kind of like winning in a team sport—everyone shares in the victory because they contributed in some way.

Through the course of the semester, the teachers attended four presentations by other practitioners and consultants. In each response I read, teachers made direct application to the classroom and even reported on successfully using new strategies in subsequent journal entries.

Responding to Professional Reading

In Ann Twigg's response to Cris Tovani's book *I Read It But I Don't Get It*, she shows how quickly a teacher can identify a "disconnect" and decide to make changes in practice:

> Her [the author's] honesty is refreshing. Despite my feelings on cheating, her account of her "book reports" made me smile and wonder how many students I've had . . . who have done the same thing. It even made me wonder if I ever did it. I can't remember! How heartbreaking it must have been for her to hear her teacher say she wasn't a good enough reader. I'm ashamed to say I haven't thought much about my students' past reading lives and how many of them are "fake-readers." My white picket fence world always envisions my students with heads in books . . . ready to discuss during . . . reading/writing workshop. Yes, my fence has to be repaired weekly. I've always leaned more toward the excuse[s] of laziness, chaotic lives, and lack of parenting. I grew up running the meadows with Laura Ingalls and solving mysteries with Nancy Drew. How can anyone not enjoy reading?
>
> Ding-dong! Maybe they can't read, Ann! After reading the first chapter, I quickly realized how I need to change some things. I had two "hodge-podge" tenth grade classes first semester, and I so much wish I had read this book before. . . . I probably can still name my "fake-readers" from those two classes. I remember answering their questions to *Ellen Foster* when they wouldn't (or should I type *couldn't*?) discuss what was happening in the novel. . . . I did the same thing the teacher [in the book] did with Lisa. . . . We read Bradstreet's "Upon the Burning of Our House," and [I] asked them to take annotated notes in the margins. . . . As I walked around, some had underlined a few things. . . . Many had blank pages. I went to the overhead and showed them my own. It was then that their pencils/pens went flying. Oh, how I should have approached that differently.

Will Ann approach her second semester students the same way after reading this book and reflecting on her practice? I'd say certainly not.

In her final presentation for the graduate course in which she read Tovani's book, Ann showed numerous student examples of increased comprehension based on strategies she used, like annotating or marking the text that she described in the above journal entry. Not only was

Ann learning about her teaching, her students were learning more about active reading and were becoming more capable readers. Sharon Cunningham, a teacher in the same course, had this to say after reading chapters one and two of the same book. Notice how she sets goals for herself and her students in this entry:

> Applying the concepts of a book club to a classroom setting made so much sense. I guess I have done this unintentionally from time to time but not systematically. If students come to class realizing they must depend on each other to construct meaning, they may not feel as threatened. . . . Small literature circles that converge with the whole class to share would be an ideal setting. By asking questions and drawing inferences the students will begin to grasp the plot. By revisiting and rethinking sections . . . the students will become better readers instead of [better] word-callers. . . .
>
> I definitely want to adapt the Important Book and Literary Histories form to my instruction. I will change it somewhat to focus on the purpose of the students' reading. . . .
>
> I applaud Tovani's honesty with her students. I, too, was not a strong reader as a student. My love of reading developed later. . . . I will share my distaste for forced reading. I will let them know they are not alone. My goal is to make SSR a rewarding experience for each student. I'm tired of seeing the daydreamers, fakers, and sleepers. I have . . . resistive readers and word-callers. . . . Is this laziness or have we programmed them to think (or not to think) this way?
>
> My final point: Tovani says "avoid pressures to cover content." Who is in charge of the Essential Reading List . . . ? I will spend only enough time on the ERL to prepare my students for the EOC [End of Course Test]. . . . I will choose more enticing selections for my students. I am going to say "no" to anything that does not directly benefit . . . my students or me. There. I think that covers it for today. . . .

Sharon shows again how the professional reading changed her instructional planning in this journal entry completed more than halfway through the book and our course:

> I understand Tovani's "sense of panic" when she realizes that her students don't care if their reading makes sense or not. I scan the room during SSR and see the "dead eyes." I've tried various techniques with

my "No thank you, I'd rather not" readers, but I realize now . . . I have not strategically applied my strategies. When [Jason] says, "Why would I reread when I didn't like it the first time?" I realize I need a plan. I remember in college trudging through . . . history texts. . . . I . . . was dying. I could see the light—and it wasn't at the end of the tunnel. After three pages I was already gravitating to the light. . . . Rereading almost killed me.

Now that I'm implementing a strategy of fix-up plans, I see some progress with . . . my struggling readers. . . . We began *Ellen Foster* with several prereading activities. [Bobby] connected a little too much. He started with a story about his father's abusive treatment. . . . Before I could slow him down, he was telling another. . . . His parents made him go [to church] . After arriving . . . he stole a child's wheelchair and drove it home!

I am creating a weekly reading log that focuses on a different strategy each day. . . . We practiced with double-entry diaries last week. Surprisingly this was a new activity for many students. Connecting and visualizing work nicely together. Our students are such visual learners that I can understand . . . I need to work on an activity connecting the two.

Professional reading, when combined with written and verbal reflection, results in changed teaching. It is one of the best and most economical investments we can make in teachers' growth.

Venting Frustrations

Several years ago during my doctoral study at the Chabad Academy, one teacher who participated wrote this after reflecting upon a parent-teacher conference night. It is perhaps one of the best examples of venting I've ever read:

Conferencing—the purpose: to discuss students' attributes and problem areas with their parents. The actuality: hearing 80 percent of twenty-three parents' problems with personal items . . . physical ailments, and parenting. . . . While calmly listening and nodding (while keeping one eye on the clock) . . . and firmly informing them that no, I will not tell the other teachers how they should run their classrooms, I bite my tongue from suggesting they order a lifetime subscription to [a] parenting magazine. . . .

She was certainly blowing off steam here, but isn't it wonderful for teachers to have the safe outlet of doing so in a private journal?

Middle-school teacher Wanda Freeman vented her frustrations by writing an unsent editorial. Here is part of her letter.

> I found a copy of your editorial on the table in our workroom, you know, the place all new teachers are warned to stay out of for fear of being jaded and discouraged by the veteran masters of discontent. . . .
>
> I am angry. I am angry with myself. I am angry with those whom I consider my bosses, near and far. I am angry with my students.
>
> I am angry with myself because I have not found courage to stand and say, "Divided no more!" . . . I have not stopped to search for and find strength in who I am and . . . what I believe. In *Teaching Other People's Children*, Cynthia Ballenger wrote of the Haitian proverb: "If you can't go to war yourself, send the plume of your hat." . . . The plume of your hat is a great addition to the effort if that's all you can manage . . . I have not sent my plume. I have only sighed about what I do not have to give. . . .
>
> I am angry at my bosses, near and far, because they have turned tail and run, leaving me to work like a dog to make them look good. . . . [They] do not share my vision of what is good for struggling readers and writers. . . . We have jumped on another bandwagon that promises to raise PACT scores but makes no mention of raising students' desire and ability to read and write. I am angry because I feel I am getting better at manual labor, hefting reams and reams of used paper, carrying them back and forth . . . down an assembly line without really paying attention to the end result.
>
> I am angry with my students because they are satisfied knowing what little they do know and are satisfied to just coast along. . . .
>
> It just seems too simple and we make it so hard. I need to learn more strategies and do more research and plan better lessons. My bosses need . . . to see that simple is better. My students need to understand that reading and writing are . . . joys that can take them to places . . . their video games and televisions cannot. I will stop venting when things start happening. . . .
>
> Until then, I remain, A Teacher in the Throes of Professional Growth.

Teachers who reflect, as Wanda does here, abound. We need only to listen to them and to use their vented frustrations to improve our schools.

Affirming and Celebrating One's Teaching

Olga Toggas, a novice teacher, deservedly patted herself on the back when she wrote this in her teaching journal: "I modeled an inference activity on chapter 6 of *The Pearl* after Jan's demonstration [in the graduate class] with *Rose Blanche.* When I put my students into groups to 'say something,' they were able to provide all sorts of clarity for each other."

In another journal entry, Olga affirms her teaching because it is aligned with what she is reading in a professional book: "I use many of the access tools mentioned on a daily basis. Most often, I do think-alouds and allow my students to see me struggling." How exciting to be fairly new to the profession and to be using innovative methods with success.

Cathy Threatt affirms her own pedagogical beliefs and her teaching abilities in this journal entry:

> Obviously, some pieces of [literature] are easier to connect than others, but it is worth the extra work to help my struggling students "get it." Also this year more than ever I have utilized read-alouds in my class. I know I have already mentioned this, but Jan [another teacher] and I made up a worksheet for the children's book *Rose Blanche.* We used this for [South Carolina] exit exam review for inference, and we used it to discuss WWII. The students loved it, and it was a neat experience for me. My kids told me I should teach history—you know, because history only consists of WWII!

Cathy was using read-alouds to enhance the other literature she was teaching in her classes, and her students responded well. This made her feel more effective, and as she notes, the whole experience was positive. Having kept in contact with Cathy, I know she continues to expand and tweak her use of read-alouds with her high school English students.

Journal Formats and Possibilities

The word "journal" naturally suggests the act of writing, but I would like to encourage the use of verbal and electronic journals as well.

Although I am just now starting to study these alternate forms in my own work, I believe they hold real potential.

By a "verbal" journal, I mean a focused conversation, perhaps in response to a writing prompt. In my work over a three-year period with the faculty of the Chabad Academy we often started meetings with journal writing. Invariably, however, a few people arrived late and missed some or all of the allotted writing time. If they chose to respond when others were sharing from their journals, the latecomers' responses were spontaneous and oral as opposed to originating in the written word. One of our best meetings ensued when we all wrote about an influential teacher, either in a positive or negative way. As teachers entered into the discussion (some of whom had not written because they were not there at that time), the discussion became more animated. Everyone wanted to tell the story of a most loved, most hated, or most revered teacher. I steered the conversation toward discussing how our significant teacher(s) helped make us the teachers we grew to be. It was a rich, productive discussion, and each teacher's verbal response (storytelling, actually) was like an oral journal entry.

Electronic (or online) journals are now fairly common. My last doctoral class in 2000 required each student to post one response per week on an electronic bulletin board for all to read and to discuss in the next class. While I have not yet used this type of electronic journal with my graduate students, I have recently experimented with e-mail journals. The teachers in the last class I taught (a class about teaching literature in the secondary school) were required to send a group e-mail once a week to everyone enrolled. They were to respond to the professional reading we were doing in addition to other class assignments. The e-mails were a joy for me to read and offered colleagues ideas about strategies to try, support for things not going well, and recommendations of further reading. I would like to continue using e-mail, discussion list, and bulletin board–type journals in the future and study how the electronic medium affects the responses. My graduate students last semester commented on the ease of the format, and the entries certainly did not lack depth or reflection. Electronic formats are rich for exploration, and I look forward to using them more in the future.

CLASSROOM RESEARCH

Fourteen teachers enrolled in a classroom inquiry course I taught in the fall of 2000. My own research question was, "How can I encourage collaboration and community among English teachers at my school?" As an assistant principal, I wanted to nurture reflection and experimentation in a nonsupervisory way. The strategy that worked best with my research question was having informal breakfast meetings about once every six weeks. I would send out a provocative professional article or question and invite teachers to come to talk and eat. I did not track the data in any systematic way, but the discussions were good, and I made sure to follow up by finding resources or dropping in on teachers during their planning periods between the meetings.

The teachers completed an inquiry planning form for me early in the course, and the other instructor and I coached them throughout the process. Here is an abbreviated version of what appeared on the form:

1. Your inquiry question (Example: How do I get my students to revise their writing instead of just edit it?)
2. Professional resources you will use (Example: Barry Lane's book *After the End*)
3. Teaching strategies you will try (Example: Barry Lane's snapshots, thoughtshots, explode the moment)
4. Data you will examine (Example: drafts of students' writing, notes from a peer observer, my own reflective journal entries)
5. Expected results or goals (Example: Students will have more vivid details in their writing. Students will be able to articulate the differences between revision and editing.)
6. Importance of results and goals (Say why this study is important to you and your students.)
7. Ideas for your presentation (What will you share with other teachers?)
8. Possible collaborators at your school

The following were all real questions developed by teachers in the course: How can I get first graders to use more details in their writing?

How do I get my students to expand their spoken and written vocabularies? How can I assist students in developing more confidence in their writing? How do I get my students to read as writers—to connect literature study with their personal writing? How do I get second graders to revise their writing better? How can I teach ESOL students to read better through their own writing? What activities promote reading enjoyment as well as increased comprehension? How do I make writing a natural, accepted part of my art classes?

The teachers studied their questions over several months, reading related professional literature, using new teaching methods, watching students carefully, and analyzing different sources of data. At the end of the course, each teacher did a forty-five-minute, conference-quality presentation for his peers to explain his project and show results.

Promoting such inquiry at any school is not hard, but it does require organization and commitment. Teachers may select two or three inquiry questions per year, and they should naturally evolve, not be mandated from above.

OBSERVATIONS

An observation-coaching cycle *in addition to any required evaluation process* is beneficial for the observed and the observer. For the observed teacher, observations and follow-up conversations illuminate practice. If the observer is an administrator, observations provide real data about what is going on in classrooms day in and day out. The follow-up conversations allow for purposeful talk focused upon the teaching act.

Supporting Excellence

Excellent teachers need to be observed more often than the times when we are trying to "show them off" to school board members or other visitors. I remember during my eighth year of teaching, the faculty selected me Teacher of the Year at my school, an honor I took very seriously and was proud of. However, I also remember being a bit resentful because the administrators never really came into my room to *see* what I was doing; they simply thought I was wonderful based on word of mouth from other teachers, my self-sufficiency and positive attitude, and the low number of discipline referrals I wrote.

Emily Morton, whom you read about earlier in this book, is an excellent teacher. I worked with nine teachers at Emily's school last year and tried to spend a fairly equal amount of time coaching each one, but in Emily's case, I felt that there was little I could do. She was already doing a fantastic job. Below are two examples of written feedback I provided for her after visiting her classes. The first is from August, when I was brand new and was transcribing madly in everyone's classes in order to better understand each unique teaching situation. The second is from January, after the two of us had been together at least one class period and one individual coaching session per week. Notice the conversational tone I take with her and the sincere praise I offer.

Dear Emily,

Once again, it was my pleasure to be with your class this morning. I got to break in my new teaching journal and jotted some things down as I participated in your class.

I will look for *The Handbook of Poetic Forms* and share it with you. You may want to teach some of the specialized forms. For example, not only is haiku explained in there, but also another form of Japanese poetry called tanka. I've taught both of these in writing workshops before, and they work well. You can look at the book, and if you want to work with students to write these kinds of poems or any others, we can teach the lessons together.

I enjoyed looking at your book *The Treasury of Quotations for Children.* Do other teachers in the department know about this resource? I bet it's great for your "food for thought" mini-lessons and also for writing prompts.

You are repeatedly using PACT terminology with the children, like "open response." Good. They will know just what that means come test time.

I love the story "Thank You, M'am." One of my favorites. Thank you. I also thought it was wonderful that you had the students draw their reactions to the story. You were once again tapping into multiple intelligences and learning preferences. If a child can't learn in your room, I don't know where he or she can! You do such a good job of having the kids tap into all their senses as they tackle the lessons.

See you again soon.

Dear Emily,

As always, it was my pleasure to be with you and your students this morning. Thank you for involving me in the assignments! I always enjoy reading and writing with your classes.

The way you are reviewing the reading pretest is wonderful—small doses, interactive, reflective. Also, you are the master of teaching voice. I wish I could bottle you and sell you; we'd both be millionaires!

Do me a favor and e-mail me a list of your "top ten" (like David Letterman) authors who show strong voice. I would put Cynthia Rylant on my list for sure. I bet you'd have Jack Prelutsky. Can you come up with eight more so I can recommend them to the department? (I will not use your name when I send out the list if you prefer I don't.)

The way you are reviewing the PACT writing rubric is good, too. They will surely internalize the important points after you have them look at that rubric and talk about it every week between now and the first week of May.

I will see you in our meeting at 1:30 Thursday in Antoine's room and in the department meeting Thursday after school in your room. We will certainly be tired of looking at each other on Thursday, won't we? Keep the faith!

For an example of how I transcribed a short visit to an excellent high school English teacher's class and also used a required observation instrument, see appendix F. These are the actual notes I took while I was in the class for approximately fifteen minutes. Note that on the observation checklist form, I made a suggestion: Consider making your classroom library easier to get to for students. The teacher and I had a brief conversation about this the very next day as I was circulating through the halls. He had received my written feedback and approached me for my ideas about how to rearrange his classroom furniture and materials.

Documenting Incompetence

Doing classroom observations was my favorite part of being an assistant principal for curriculum. The classroom is where everything important happens in a school, and I like to roll up my sleeves and get in there every chance I get. Sadly, I had to roll up my sleeves and do a lot of work with poor teachers. In a school of over 100 faculty members, someone in administration must assist the principal in making sound judgments about the quality of instruction, and in this case, that responsibility fell mainly to me for four years.

In one case, I began observing and coaching a new teacher in hopes of supporting him and helping him grow to competence. He also had a mentor teacher assigned to him as part of the state's required evaluation system. She and I met with him twice in his first month of teaching and were feeling pretty positive until we began observing. He had no control. The sophomore students were literally walking all over him—walking all over the room, walking out the door, etc. The lessons he had planned were sound; he just could not get students to comply with classroom rules. I noticed that in one-on-one conversations with students, he was very caring, helpful, and knowledgeable. However, when a one-on-one conference was taking place, twenty or so other students in the room were way off task. The situation was chaotic bordering on dangerous.

His mentor and I met with him repeatedly, giving him concrete suggestions to implement. I would observe and find that the suggestions stopped being effective after one or two class periods. He simply could not "stick to his guns." I also asked the special education inclusion teacher assigned to many of his students to be in his classes as many times a week as possible.

I had to move from a coaching stance to a supervisory one. I began to observe several times a week, and whereas before I was assisting with students and helping to manage the class, I had to pull back unless a dangerous situation occurred. It was now time to document his incompetence.

I had several meetings with him (minus the mentor teacher) and sternly told him what had to happen. He had to gain control. He had to teach his content and prevent disruptions. Plus, he had to learn to do this *alone*. No one was going to coteach with him if he stayed in the profession. He had received a great bonus by having both me and the inclusion teacher present for as much time as we had been already.

After several more meetings and much soul-searching on his part, he decided he would resign over the Thanksgiving break. This was the right thing to do for him personally and professionally, and above all, it was the right thing to do for the students. We had the chance to hire a December graduate from a local university, and she very capably handled his teaching assignment for the remainder of the year.

Another teacher, a veteran of over twenty-five years, was in the process of being denied a contract based on her failure to pass the required evaluation in addition to two years of detailed observations and meetings with me. She opted for retirement instead of going through the battles that were sure to ensue. In the year that I knew we would push for dismissal, my documentation began with a memo written after only a ten-minute observation. More details about this particular case appear in appendix G.

Questioning Mediocrity

The most rewarding work for me is helping teachers who are "in the middle"—not outstanding, not horrible, but on the verge of being really effective. Using observations, transcripts, and coaching with them produces real change.

Below is the text of written feedback I offered to a teacher after observing and assisting in her room several times. She was really struggling with one class. (I transcribed notes in her classes between times I was assisting and used these notes to write the feedback. I did not provide the notes to her at the time because I thought she would get discouraged.)

Notice how I am trying to help her plan lessons integrating literature and grammar, something she was not doing effectively yet. This note to her began a yearlong discussion of lesson planning that later turned into her taking the lead and feeling greater confidence.

Bravo for you! I think it's great that you're thinking "out of the box" about your class. I know they will learn more as you tailor instruction to better suit their needs.

Your student got my book to you. [The media specialist] is also finding other books for you today and will put them in your box (great stuff for read-alouds).

Monday, explain to your class how they will be doing different, "cooler" work. You could even give a different journal prompt for them, maybe something like "write about a time you were misunderstood" or "write about a time you got blamed for something that wasn't your fault." (These topics fit in well with the story.) You could have them write for ten minutes and then a few students could share out loud. This would set the stage for your read-aloud.

After reading the book to them, discuss the terms protagonist and antagonist and discuss the two versions of the story. They could work in pairs to generate a list of qualities of antagonists and protagonists. Maybe they could name characters from cartoons and movies that fit the definitions. Give them a few minutes and then have each group "report out."

I would suggest that you photocopy my book. Then, on Monday (or Tuesday if you run out of time Monday), you could break students into groups of four, and give each group a photocopied page or two. Make sure there are at least two types of sentences on the section you give each group. Have each group go through its assigned sentences and classify them by the four types. (The hardest ones to find are imperative, but there are some there.)

You could also choose from the "revised" fairy tales from the library book to reinforce the concept of protagonist/antagonist.

Then, on Wednesday, you could do the lesson on nouns followed by a read-aloud from any book you choose. You could use the photocopied pages again and have them identify nouns from what you just read.

I'll do my book project this weekend, too, to help model for your students. Tell me when to come to your classes to share it. I wasn't sure when you'd give them the assignment. My stuff is flexible. Let me know!

Another teacher I have worked with recently came to teaching after another career and is unfamiliar with many good resources. Notice how in this written feedback I offer her books to turn to:

I enjoy collaborating with you and appreciate the opportunity to work so closely with your class. I'm excited about how the positive/negative graph will work. I'm also glad you thought the "who are you?" activity may be fruitful.

I'd love to look at some of the writing you get as a result of these prompts. Then we could see where to go next with the students. We could find strengths to build upon and weaknesses to better support.

The positive/negative graph is from Linda Rief's book *Seeking Diversity*. Nancie Atwell's *In the Middle* also has a useful activity called "writing territories." The "who are you?" thing I just made up on my own somehow. I have other prompts that seem to work well for lots of different audiences. I'll try to pull them for you if you're interested.

I'd like to talk about [the fall remediation class] when we know more about it. I think an engaging read-aloud with some connected activities would be a good way to start each day.

I'll be back with you at about 11:00 Friday. See you later! Keep smiling!

Both of these examples come from a school I have served in a coaching capacity. As a coach for instructional improvement, I am often assisting or demonstrating when I'm in the classroom, so I do not do as much "straight" transcription as I did when I was in the supervisory role of assistant principal. I now transcribe mostly for my own journals, so that I can look back over each week and decide what teachers need me to do to support them and help them grow.

PROFESSIONAL READING AND PROFESSIONAL CONFERENCES

Both of these tools have been discussed adequately earlier in the chapter; however, I can't resist sharing this response Wanda Freeman wrote after attending a conference where she met one of her teaching "idols," writer and educator Ralph Fletcher:

The most significant thing to my learning was meeting and listening to Ralph Fletcher. I guess it's like kids meeting their favorite athlete or music star. I ate up everything and was encouraged by the fact that he feels the same way I do about what is important in teaching. To see someone who is famous for their craft be so approachable and have valuable lessons and advice to offer is uplifting. At any conference, I relish the camaraderie I feel when I am with people who feel as I do about most things important to me. Because I have been out of the loop, it was good for me just to get back to what I love, conferring with others who have made guru status.

RESPONSE QUESTIONS FOR CHAPTER 4

1. If you are a teacher, think about the last time another adult came into your classroom as you were teaching. What was the purpose of the visit? How would you feel if a colleague or supervisor observed you and transcribed a lesson?

2. If you are an administrator, think about how you could add observations with follow-up to the regular routine at your school. How can you "open up" the teaching act to scrutiny in order for your teachers to improve? How can you best support your exemplary teachers while also encouraging mediocre teachers to improve? How can you begin to force incompetent teachers to change or leave the profession? Who can help you in this mission?

CHAPTER 5

Inside-Out as a Contributing Professional

"Our deepest calling is to grow into our own authentic selfhood. . . . As we do so, we will not only find the joy that every human being seeks—we will also find our path of authentic service in the world. True vocation joins self and service. . . ."

—Parker Palmer in *Let Your Life Speak*

The distinction between the concepts of "vocation" and "occupation" is important. There is nothing more satisfying in this world, aside from the joy of loving and spending time with one's family, than being engaged in fulfilling work. True gratification in one's work makes a profession more than just a job and makes life more enjoyable.

Some teachers are in the profession because it is a steadily paying job with good benefits, not because they hear the voice of fulfilling vocation. (My idealistic self likes to think that there are very few of these people.) However, once a teacher has been involved in good professional development, I hope she has come to a new sense of fulfillment about her chosen field. Surely she has come to understand herself better as both a learner and as a teacher of and role model for other learners. She is still on a journey of continuous learning, however, and with that journey comes additional responsibility. Teachers who have grown and changed as professionals must add to their repertoire ways of giving back—service to the teaching community, if you will. This is how we become contributors to the profession of teaching. It is more than networking, which sometimes serves only the person's own best interests; it is actually *feeling responsible* for and *making contributions* to the development of other teachers.

Teaching is a profession—one of the hardest, most underpaid, most unappreciated, and, at its core, one of the most creative. There is creativity in service.

A prerequisite for being a contributor is to be a reader of the work of other professionals. You cannot give back to the learning community if you don't know what's being talked about, published, and read. You must be familiar with the contributions your colleagues are making through their public works.

You may be saying to yourself, this woman wants me to think about my own thinking, reexperience subject matter, and now stay aware of current professional literature, too? Just when am I supposed to do this? At midnight after all my papers are graded, my kids are in bed, and my spouse has drifted off? No. Reading professional materials can be interwoven into your already busy day, and I contend that if you do not read professional materials, you are doing a disservice to both yourself and your profession.

Lieberman (2000) touts "embedded" staff development, and reading relevant materials is both personalized and embedded—meaning you have choice in selecting the materials, and you can do it at your work site. Administrators must value professional reading. However, take it upon yourself to value it even if your supervisors don't. Make staying informed a priority. You will be working smarter, not harder. You will be a more astute educator, and you can achieve this status relatively easily during work hours or during other routine activities. For example, if you have a duty-free lunch, a couple of times a week, read for fifteen minutes while you're nibbling. You can read a book of actual pages or surf some of the best Internet sites. In your teacher's planning book or your daily calendar, pencil this in and vow not to let an irate parent, last-minute request from a supervisor, or rehearsal for the school play preempt it. Isn't reading two times a week for fifteen minutes a better use of time than participating in the latest round of gossip in the teachers' lounge? Another idea: if you're taking a holiday car trip and your spouse does some of the driving, pack a new professional book and set a goal to read it along the way. Better yet, keep a professional book in the car with you at all times. (See chapter 7 and the appendices for my recommendations.) When a traffic jam strikes, you're prepared to use your time wisely. Take the book with you into the Division of Motor Vehicles, doctor appointments, parent-teacher conference nights, and any place where you may experience a wait. I finish about one professional book a month just by having it handy and perusing it in these otherwise wasted moments spent waiting, waiting, waiting. Also make it a goal to subscribe to at least one professional journal and read a lead article the very first day you get it in the mail. I do this as soon as I come in with the mail in hand. I know if I wait, I will procrastinate. I actually look forward to choosing the one article I'll attack immediately! Try these tips and see if they don't help you become a more frequent reader and, by doing so, a more competent professional.

Joining professional organizations and networks provides you with new ideas and allows you to take part in good conferences at reduced rates. By attending conferences, you'll meet like-minded professionals and engage in collegial conversation. Make a pledge to yourself to attend at least one professional conference a year *on a topic that is important to you.* Many times, schools and districts have paid-for slots to fill at workshops and conferences and don't give much thought to whom to send until the last minute. Whether you are a teacher or administrator, *avoid this last-minute decision-making at all costs.* Very rarely do last-minute fill-ins get as much from a conference as they could. A school's staff should be strategic in planning who will attend what and budget for it in the summer prior to the new year. Many state and local conferences occur year after year in the same place and at roughly the same time of year. Plan for these yourself and approach the person who approves the expenditures within the first few weeks of school. In my experience, budgets are often withered up by March, and no one can go anywhere in April and May, so plan ahead. It pays.

Pursuing advanced study is another way to grow professionally and to contribute to the growth of other professionals. Again, *choose wisely.* Take graduate courses that get positive word-of-mouth reviews either because the content is especially engaging, the instructor is good, or a combination of both. Avoid what is merely convenient, like online courses, if you don't feel they will meet your needs. (I have found that courses hyping "convenience" are usually very expensive as well.) Professionals need relevance, immediate applicability, and collaboration. Make sure what you sign up for has these components. Once you are enrolled and are participating in a class, take time to talk with others, especially younger or less experienced teachers. Remind your-self to talk with them about the positives of being an educator; we all hear enough negativity each day at work. Be a role model of the reflec-tive, continuously learning teacher, not the tired, know-it-all one who is counting the days until summer vacation.

Take it upon yourself to share best practices, both informally and formally. If you are an administrator, provide ways to do this. (See chapter 6 for suggestions.) If you are a department chair or other teacher-leader, provide time *at each and every meeting* to highlight at least one successful instructional practice. Turn your department mem-bers into presenters. Each person can be told at the beginning of the school year, "You will take ten minutes of our department meeting to present something that has worked well in your classroom. Be ready!" Too many meetings get mired in trivial conversation. Take it upon yourself as a participant in any meeting to help steer the conversation toward instructional issues.

Whether you are a teacher or an administrator, write and present suc-cessful lessons or ideas. There are many ways to publish on the Internet in addition to the more traditional print publications. Apply to present at conferences held in your area. When I was in my first few years of teaching, I would apply to present at everything within a sixty-mile radius. I figured if I got accepted and the principal knew she would get the school's name in the program, she would have to pay for me to attend! As a result, I became involved in two wonderful professional organizations, became a more skilled presenter, met energetic col-leagues, and discovered hundreds of teaching ideas and resources.

STORIES: TEACHERS BECOMING FULL CONTRIBUTORS TO THE PROFESSION

Let's revisit Gretchen Meier, middle-school language arts teacher who just completed her fifth year, a person I've known and taught since she was an undergraduate. Gretchen has moved from being a neophyte into the stage where I'd say she is becoming an accomplished veteran.

Here is Gretchen, telling her own story:

Before the writing project, I taught two years . . . and hated it [at the school where I was]. There was no collaboration and they paid very little attention to first year teachers. I did a one-week workshop with Connie Prevatte . . . but nothing ever came of it, except that we were required to do the four-block [literacy] method. I hated that too. . . . Let's not quote that experience; I'm trying to forget it! The problem with [the school] is that they did not put any effort into their new teachers and had a horrible retention rate. Is that why teachers left, because they didn't put any effort into them or do they not put any effort into them because they know they are going to leave? It's a double-edged sword, I guess.

Now I'm at Myrtle Beach Middle School, and I love it. Here they encourage working together; in fact, they strongly encourage it and ask us to plan together during our planning period. I think it's also easier to work and collaborate with people when you like them, and I really like my coteachers here. We respect each other. I think I have also become more collaborative because I have taken so many classes and attended so many conferences that I feel much more open to sharing what I have. Prior to that, I think I was still so green that I was afraid to share my ideas. Even though I knew I had good ideas, I didn't know how open people would be to a new teacher coming in with new ideas. I didn't want to seem like I was coming in and trying to change a successful curriculum. . . . Sometimes you have to feel people out. You have to pay your dues. . . . I think you have to wait a little before charging up the ladder.

I now am the [district] teacher liaison at the . . . meetings once a month. . . . I have given presentations for you and at our school and [our department chair] said she wants me to be department chair next year but I don't know if that will happen. This is really exciting! I have also been asked to sit on the committee for the state department of education to help create the new ELA Middle Level Praxis test. . . . I had a practicum student but never a student teacher, but this year we had a new 8th grade ELA teacher and I . . . was her unofficial mentor.

I think the work I have done has helped me a great deal not only in my classroom but also in my school because so many teachers haven't taken a class or been to a conference in years, and so I am able to be the one they come to if they want anything new. I usually run the department meetings and fill them in on what they need to know. But the funny thing is that I don't consider myself a teacher-leader. It's just something I do because I enjoy being in the know and most other people don't have time. I think also people don't bother to come to ask for a lot because they are pleased with the way their classrooms run, so they tend not to try too many new things. You know who I am talking about—"why fix what ain't broken" kind of teachers. No desire for any new ideas. Ugh, they drive me nuts!

You asked how I have become increasingly sure of myself as a leader, and I don't know that I have. Put me in front of Ann Twigg or Janet Files . . . and I don't know that I would feel very sure of myself or my teaching. I know that I have a large base of knowledge now . . . but I would never put my teaching up against theirs. I think it's just because they have more experience and years of proven results, and we got yelled at for two years of drops in PACT scores. . . . I know that I have good knowledge but a lot of times my confidence lacks. You know the expression: overt self-confidence masking serious insecurities. That's me. I am proud of what I've done . . . but I still feel so green sometimes that I hesitate to say I'm sure of myself. Maybe it's like Janet used to say when I was student teaching, that it's healthy tension, but through all the classes and conferences and ideas, I still worry every day that I'm not doing the best darn job I can. Am I really giving everything I can? Do I really care enough? Am I giving them all the tools they need to be successful? I worry and sometimes I just have to throw my hands up or else I would worry myself sick.

I want to be one of those amazing teachers and right now I feel I am just a good teacher. I do know that because I want to be better that I can have it, because I will continue to try to grow. . . . And I guess that when I stop worrying, that's when I should leave the classroom because teachers need to want to continue to improve. If they don't, how can they stand in front of a group of kids and ask them to grow?

Gretchen shows rising confidence as she becomes increasingly knowledgeable and collaborative. Being in a school environment that encourages professional growth and frequent collaboration has served her well. I like to think that completing four graduate courses with me has nurtured her, too, but of course, she would not have grown and changed without the desire to do so and without knowing the benefits she would reap.

You have read excerpts from Frank Clark's journal in earlier chapters. Frank is fifty-three years old and has been teaching for seventeen years. He currently teaches U. S. history, government, and psychology at a school for juniors and seniors who also major in a particular field of career study. In the summer of 2001, Frank took the Writing Project. The following fall, he took a graduate course for secondary teachers in teaching composition. In his own words, he demonstrates how this collaboration helped him remain positive about his vocation:

> I have always enjoyed school and people, but fell into teaching after college and a year of travel, plus three years of menial jobs. I thought about leaving for the restaurant business, but as I gained experience and confidence, I realized it was a good profession for me. I also prayed for guidance and the Lord never seemed to want me to change vocations.
>
> So much of professional development is not development as much as cramming policy down your throat or developing as the district dictates, not what you as a professional feel you need. There have been some good opportunities of late that I have taken advantage of, including the "We the People" institute last summer. . . . Sometimes it is not the district that is at fault but teachers who don't want to spend time really learning from others.
>
> The Writing Project was an excellent experience for me. I was able to focus on writing and working with a group of dedicated, talented teachers. The sharing, bonding, and positive criticisms were priceless for me personally, and for my development as an accomplished teacher of creative expression. As I read over my journal I was proud, but upset that I have not written much lately. It is time to resume.

Frank is still taking part in workshops, seminars, and conferences and is reflecting on his professional growth continuously. Like Gretchen, he works in a school that nurtures him as a professional by requiring that he collaborate with colleagues on a regular basis, not only about instruction but about student behavior issues as well. He works as part of an interdisciplinary team (something rare in high schools) and feels that he is making worthwhile contributions not only to his students but also to his peers.

RESPONSE QUESTIONS FOR CHAPTER 5

1. List three positive things about being a teacher. How can you share these positives with other teachers?

2. Who has contributed to your growth and satisfaction in teaching? Professors, mentors in the schools in which you've worked, teachers who have written professional books, presenters? Write about one of these influential people. What would you like to thank this person for?

CHAPTER 6

Notes for Supervisors

"The best minute I spend is the one I invest in people."

—Kenneth Blanchard and Spencer Johnson in
The One-Minute Manager

"Truly, believing is seeing. We must, therefore, seek to believe in the unseen potential."

—Stephen Covey in *Principle-Centered Leadership*

Encouraging introspection and collaboration is not easy for today's educational leaders. As demands grow exponentially, budgets shrink. Personnel and materials must be used in nontraditional, cost-effective ways. However, thinking, reading, writing, and talking do not cost much. The leader committed to improving instruction through inside-out professional development does not have to acquire new funding but does have to use existing funding and personnel creatively. (Suggestions are made later in this chapter.)

As a supervisor, there are many roles one plays: coach, cheerleader, friend, parent, role model, teacher, disciplinarian, and so on. When I was an assistant principal, I liked some of the hats I wore and disliked others. When I had to take the parent or disciplinarian stance with adults, I knew I was changing the school for the better, but I would have rather been helping teachers design effective lessons or planning the next inservice for the faculty.

Likewise, teachers wear many hats throughout their careers and take different stances with administrators depending on personality type, time, situation, and mood. I have already mentioned that I once considered myself a trailblazer but now am more of a pioneer (Schlechty

1993). Each faculty has within it trailblazers, pioneers, settlers, stay-at-homes, saboteurs, and all sorts of characters in between. Novice teachers often need different kinds of support than veterans of ten years or more. When faced with pressure from supervisors to make changes, teachers can take different postures. They may embrace the suggested or mandated changes and move forward (the ideal scenario). What is more common in my experience is for them to plead ignorance or be reluctant, resistant, or outright defiant.

Start slowly. Real change takes time. You want to cultivate the habits of close observation, reflection, and experimentation. You want to encourage teachers to be innovative but still hold them accountable for real results in student learning. In this time of mandate after mandate and test on top of test, asking teachers to "do one more thing" can backfire.

Survey teachers, both informally and formally. Hold discussion groups and get their ideas for staff development topics. Conduct a needs assessment if you or your school district has not already done so this year. Solicit feedback on the inservice you have already had this year. Do they feel it has been effective? If so, how? If not, what can be done?

After you have gathered some ideas, observe in classrooms. Talk with teachers about what they are teaching and how they are teaching it. Drop in on department meetings, not to talk but to listen. At a faculty meeting, have an entrance or exit slip activity (totally anonymous) in which teachers write a quick response to a question related to staff development. If you're an administrator, you could ask teachers what they want to learn more about or ask what one thing you could take off their plates in order to foster increased reflection and collaboration. *Be careful when you ask this!* You are not asking what you can do to free up more time in their day necessarily, but you are asking what you can do to encourage increased professionalism through inquiry and dialogue. If there are meetings that could be better handled via e-mail or memo, then cancel the meetings. If there are duties that interfere with teachers' planning time, could you utilize personnel or parent volunteers differently to assist with those duties? Question the constraints that you have and ask teachers to question them as well; you may come up with some creative ways to use time, space, and people's energy.

You may want to dip into the observation process (after doing some observations yourself, of course, to model what you expect) by requiring each teacher to observe a peer for one class period. How you orchestrate this is up to you. In the school where my colleagues and I did this, the principal told the faculty that each person would have to give up one planning period each semester to observe a colleague. The only guidelines for the observation were these: record your name, the name of the person you observed, and document the date and time; have the observed teacher sign off; write a couple of sentences about what you will take back to your own teaching as a result of this observation. Some people did "fake" it on the first run-through. Others chose unwisely and simply dropped in on their friends. However, by the second time around, many folks were talking about how good it was to actually see someone else teaching and to get useful ideas right there in their own building. If you try some informal observations like this, be forewarned: some people will try to hoodwink you. But don't give up. As my friend and role model Paul Browning says, don't penalize 100 percent of the people for something only 10–20 percent of them are doing; take care of the 10–20 percent instead. Good advice that works with both teachers and students.

Remember Goethe's famous words as you begin to plan better staff development: "Things which matter most must never be at the mercy of things which matter least."

Before you begin observing with feedback, keep in mind one of the most valuable lessons I have learned from Kenneth Blanchard and Spencer Johnson: give criticism sandwiched between two sincere compliments. Granted, sometimes it's hard to dig down and come up with those compliments, but it can be done. The two teachers I discussed in the section on documenting incompetence in chapter 4 had some real strengths that I did not fail to mention. The male teacher was extremely knowledgeable of his subject matter and genuinely cared for others. His concern for others was almost palpable. The female had a quirky sense of humor and developed strong rapport with some of her students. She could be quite animated when discussing great literature, making it obvious that she felt passionately about it. Despite their strengths, *neither of these people was suitable for the classroom at the time when I supervised them.* Does this make them lesser people? Certainly not. I appreciated their special qualities, but as an administrator in a public school, I had to do what I could do to provide the best education for our students.

STORIES: HOW DO I DO THIS?

In "Beyond Inservice," an article I wrote for the magazine *Principal Leadership*, I advocated the following five components of effective staff development. I'd like to revisit them and elaborate more here.

Taking Stock

Honor the individuality, identity, and integrity of teachers. Get to know them not only as teachers but as human beings.

Have icebreaker activities, silly games, and prize drawings at some faculty meetings. Have social events. Paul Browning, principal at the school where I was an assistant principal for four years, held family fishing tournaments at the local pier, faculty/family golf tournaments, and faculty cookouts every spring. After graduation and prom each year, he led a small faculty group of night owls in enjoying a little Myrtle Beach nightlife (the kids weren't the only ones celebrating on those nights!). Remember to have fun, and have some of it with the people you work with. Get to know them as more than employees.

When I work with teachers, one of the universal complaints is that "administrators don't understand." Teachers want to be treated as professionals and choose much of their own staff development. To the greatest extent possible, *let them do this*. Allow latitude and trust each person until you have reason not to trust that person. For example, I worked with a teacher once who was going to play video poker during her planning periods when she said she was "running to the bank" or "paying the electric bill." Would I trust her to have a lot of choice in her professional growth? Probably not. I would most likely not spend public funds for her to attend an out-of-town professional conference because I would not trust her to attend the sessions. However, teachers like this are few and far between. Trust and respect first; this will go a long way.

Turning Teachers into Students

Experiencing subject matter from a student's perspective informs and refreshes teachers' instructional practice. Seek out opportunities for your teachers to do this. Contact the local Writing Project director to arrange for a contract course to be taught at your site or to have her come speak with your teachers about applying to be a fellow. Hire skilled teachers to offer inquiry-reflection type courses after school, using them as the leaders. Pay them a fair stipend and award continuing education units or graduate credit. Talk with the local university's department of education faculty. See if they are interested in a joint venture designing creative new education methods courses. Encourage grant applications, especially for summer study like science camps for educators. For every grant application you receive that you think will help refresh your teachers as learners, it pays to walk that application to a teacher's room *yourself* and have a three-minute conversation. That says you care and you want to encourage them to grow.

Looking in the Mirror

Each teacher needs to see his teaching through another's eyes, or through his own eyes on videotape. This can be achieved through the observation-coaching cycle I have already discussed in many different configurations. You may have an assistant principal for curriculum and instruction; this person could logically do the bulk of observations and coaching if he does not have student discipline duties as well. You may want to divide the faculty up among administrators and take a group to observe yourself. You may want to start with teachers pairing up by choice and try a cycle of preview-observe-debrief with each other. Then after one cycle of this type, administrators could enter the mix. Some schools do only peer observations and coaching and do it quite well. However, I've found that it's best for administrators to take an active role as well. It keeps an administrator honest and real if he has to be out of the office and in classrooms, closely watching.

Showing What You Know

Have teachers share best practices. At monthly faculty meetings, you could have five presenters with short tips each time, like the "Teachers

Helping Teachers" segment we did when I was at Socastee High School. Teachers saw everything from quick demonstrations of Power Point to original board games to using music to enhance the understanding of history.

Also, orchestrate department or grade-level meetings that really matter. Meet with chairpersons at the beginning of the year—or pay them to come in and work during the summer—and tell them you expect them to be staff development leaders. In monthly meetings, they should limit discussion of administrivia (how to complete textbook forms, how to clean up the science storage closet, the parking lot duty schedule, etc.) to no more than twenty minutes. *Give them each a kitchen timer!* For the remaining thirty to forty minutes of all meetings, talk should relate to *instruction and student learning*. Use the Coalition of Essential Schools IITIC tools or any protocol or format you like, or design one yourself or along with the chairpersons. Have teachers present ideas, show student work, reflect on practice, and talk about teaching—*not* students wearing hats or chewing gum, smoking in the bathrooms, the next big fundraiser, etc.

Adding to the Toolbox

High-quality, whole-faculty inservice expands teachers' repertoires. Develop a survey instrument to assess your teachers' needs. Administer it early in the year and base most of your whole-faculty staff development on it (aside from state and district mandates).

The survey need not be the only idea generator. Base some of your whole-group inservice on what you and the other administrators see in your daily walk-arounds. Perhaps you see a lot of passive learning, like lectures. Maybe you see an overuse of videos with students not actively watching but sleeping or talking with friends instead. When such issues arise, schedule an inservice, even if only a short one. You can get a lot done in thirty minutes if you concentrate on only one or two teaching strategies, like using the jigsaw method to get students more actively involved in dry textbook material or using double-entry journals to keep students on task while watching educational videos.

Remember the tools that work with every teacher:

- journals
- classroom inquiry projects
- observations with follow-up
- professional reading
- attending professional conferences

Commit to exploring how these five components of inside-out professional development offer your teachers benefits. I have quoted Tracy Bailey earlier in this book, and I want to close this chapter with her words about participating in effective staff development during her first year of teaching. Tracy was (and is) a real dynamo, and she expresses the need for inside-out opportunities here better than I can:

> The place to improve the world is first in one's own heart, head, and hands, then work outward from there. Without professional development, teachers lose their passion for learning and their love for life. A teacher who fails to develop his full potential . . . is not only slighting the students . . . but [also] puts himself at risk of contracting the dreaded "teacheritis," . . . caused by constant tearing down and no building up. The only cure . . . is professional development and the joy that comes along with finding new and better ways to change the world.

Be the person who builds up your teachers and stamps out teacheritis at your school.

RESPONSE QUESTIONS FOR CHAPTER 6

1. If you are a teacher, what would you like to add to this chapter? Write an imaginary letter to your principal and say what you want to say about the staff development you would like to have.
2. If you are a principal, which of the five inside-out tools are you most comfortable with? How will you explore the others? How will you enhance the "building up" of your teachers this year?

CHAPTER 7

Recommendations for Further Study

"Education is not preparation for life; education is life itself."

—John Dewey

"I am neither especially clever nor especially gifted. I am only very, very curious."

—Albert Einstein

If you've made it this far with me, then you are probably convinced to enhance the "inside-outness" of professional development at your school. First, I beg you not to *call* this new direction anything. Do not walk into a meeting and say, "This year, we are going to do inside-out staff development." Really, that sounds suspect, as if you're asking everyone to wear their clothes with the labels showing, doesn't it? If you want to change staff development at your school, say little initially but instead *listen a lot.*

You've just read pages and pages of examples of improved, more focused, and responsive teaching. The teachers with whom you work can improve, become more focused and responsive, and be challenged (yet supported)—simultaneously—through meaningful staff development.

My favorite book for starting up dialogue on improved teaching is *Mind Matters: Teaching for Thinking* by Dan Kirby and Carol Kuykendall (1991). I have used sections of this book for over five years with various groups of teachers. Some chapters make for rich group reading, and there are prompts called "explorations" at the end of each chapter. These are appropriate for written or verbal response in meetings.

I also highly recommend *Classroom Instruction That Works:*

Research-Based Strategies for Increasing Student Achievement by
Robert Marzano, Debra Pickering, and Jane Pollock (2001). The
book's short chapters, summaries of research, and classroom vignettes
make it very readable and worthy of discussion.

Some of my other favorite books are by Roland Barth, Stephen
Covey, Michael Fullan, Howard Gardner, and Parker Palmer, although
they are usually not practical enough for teachers. However, because
you are an educational leader, these authors are worthy of close
reading.

Perhaps connecting your reading with a current "push" in your district or school will help get you more involved. Is it performance
assessment? Read something by Grant Wiggins or Jay McTighe. Curriculum mapping? Then look for a title by Heidi Hayes Jacobs. Data-
driven decisions? Mike Schmoker. For every topic, there are a few
authors who are considered leaders. Seek out the authors who have
something important to say on topics you are already dealing with in
your work situation. There are far too many excellent resources out
there for me to go into any detail here; I would be doing a disservice
to many others.

Commit to having a well-stocked professional library that is pleasant
and roomy enough for teachers to linger. Ask each department or grade
level to make recommendations to get you started. The Association for
Supervision and Curriculum Development should be your first stop for
professional books on a wide range of topics. Heinemann and Sten-
house publish many materials related to literacy and are worth your
time as well.

*To get started, the first purchase for every teacher and administrator
in the building should be a teaching journal.* The inexpensive composition books with marbled black and white covers work just fine. These
are usually about $1 apiece at a discount store or on clearance sale at
your local office supply vendor. If you are the principal, imagine what
kind of tone you will set if everyone gets a journal at the first faculty
meeting, and you take the time to model using it yourself.

In the school where I currently work, the principal supplied a notebook for each language arts teacher, and I pasted an inspirational poem
about teaching to the inside cover. I opened the first meeting I ever had
with them as a group by reading aloud the poem and providing a

prompt for a few minutes of journal writing time. Although I strive to make read-alouds and writing time a part of each meeting we have, I am not always successful. Perhaps in the coming year we will be able to slow down and reflect with greater frequency. Again, I will set the tone at the initial meeting and do my best from then on.

Another nice, useful gift for teachers would be *The Teacher's Daybook* by Jim Burke (2002). It's an actual planning book that incorporates written reflection and can be used as a staff development tool. The front of the book includes a "Teacher's Personal Workshop" page and a "Teacher's Professional Workshop" page that could be the basis of meaningful discussion and goal setting. Prompts include "books I want to read," "if I retired tomorrow, I would spend my time . . . ," "professional experiences I want to have," and "new subjects or texts I want to teach," among many others. There are monthly, weekly, and daily calendars, tons of tips for teachers, and reflection questions throughout. For more information on this fabulous, practical tool, log on to www.heinemann.com or Jim Burke's site, www.englishcompanion.com.

The Coalition for Essential Schools has many useful tools available to help you increase introspection, reflection, and collaboration at your school. I adapted their IITIC (Improving Instruction through Inquiry and Collaboration) protocols. Refer to figure 7.1 for copies of the actual handouts I used with graduate students one semester.

If you really want to begin this process, take the first steps yourself. If you haven't been responding to the questions at the end of each chapter of this book, flip back through and take five minutes to write an answer to just one. Tomorrow, leaf through again, and respond to another one. Any one. Your choice. Try a bit of reflective writing and see if it helps you focus on what's important at your school and respond in slightly different ways.

RESPONSE QUESTIONS FOR CHAPTER 7

1. What book will I read for myself before beginning this process with teachers? Why have I selected this book, and what do I hope to learn from it?
2. What is one thing I can do tomorrow to start encouraging greater introspection, reflection, and collaboration at my school, without telling anyone? How do I hope this action will influence others?

Think about these questions to guide your inquiry:

❑ What would you like for students to do differently? In other words, what are the results you want?
❑ What might you try to do differently in your teaching practice in order to produce the results you want?
❑ What indicators might you look for to see if what you are doing is helping to create the desired results?

What I would like to have happen . . .	I want my students to write a biographical sketch.
An obstacle to reaching this goal . . .	Some students don't know how to organize their writing.
A big question I have about this . . .	What teaching strategies will help students recognize the gaps in their own writing?
A narrower question I have about this . . .	How can I help students write better transitions?
A teaching strategy I want to try . . .	I will create a model composition and show them the effective transitions. Then I will have them self-edit and peer-edit using a sheet about transitions.
Data I could review . . . (What is the impact of——on——?)	Drafts, peer-editor comments, and self-editor comments/reflections.

Teachers must frame the inquiry in terms of the specific indicators of student achievement. To say "I want my students to write better compositions" is not enough; the specific learning is not clarified, and the data sources would be too abundant.

Types of inquiry questions that don't work well:

❑ Questions that can be answered "yes" or "no"
❑ Those that begin with "why"
❑ Those that could be easily misinterpreted
❑ Those that are too broad or too narrow
❑ Those for which the teacher already knows the answer

Types of data include:

❑ Student work (written, spoken, videotaped, audiotaped, etc.)
❑ Evidence of teacher's instructional planning and curriculum development
❑ Survey responses
❑ Written reflections (journal entries, exit slips, learning log entries, etc.)
❑ Oral interviews
❑ Anecdotal records
❑ Notes and feedback from observations of the teacher
❑ Quantitative data (grades, test scores, attendance rates, etc.)

Keeping a teaching journal is one way to record what is happening in relationship to your inquiry question. Just leave your journal somewhere in your classroom, open to a clean page each day. As you notice something that seems pertinent, jot yourself a quick note so you can recall the event. At the end of the day, at lunch time, or during your planning period, take a few minutes to jot some extended notes. If you have time, periodically look back on your jotted notes and reflect on them. Write more in-depth about these instances if possible. Your "journal jots" may guide you to new insights about your inquiry question.

Start planning your own inquiry. Here's a blank chart to get you started:

What I would like to have happen . . .	
An obstacle to reaching this goal . . .	
A big question I have about this . . .	
A narrower question I have about this . . .	
A teaching strategy I want to try . . .	
Data I could review . . . (What is the impact of———on———?)	

Arrange to be observed by a peer. The peer may take one of several different stances: she may seek to record everything that is happening; she may focus on a particular aspect, like questioning techniques; she may look for interesting moments or key events directly related to the observed teacher's inquiry question. After the observation, the two teachers should meet to debrief. The debriefing will take different forms based on the stance of the observer. (My favorite stance is the "recorder" or "camera" stance. I seek to record everything I see and hear, and then the teacher and I try to make sense of the data together.)

Figure 7.1. *How to begin teacher inquiry: Suggestions from the Coalition of Essential Schools, the Improving Instruction through Inquiry and Collaboration (IITIC) Project. Adapted by Angela Peery.*

How to Add an Inside-Out Component to Any Inservice

This appendix offers some suggestions for conducting inside-out inservice with meaningful follow-up in a variety of forums.

SHORT MEETING

Get ready ahead of time: cold drinks, light snacks like chips, nuts, or fresh fruit, warm-up activity, all handouts.

Warm-up: include movement and talking, a reconnection time; use a people-oriented bingo/scavenger hunt type activity or four corners (index card); for a quieter beginning or a smaller group, do an entrance slip or reflective journal entry (to be kept private, or orchestrate sharing time in small groups at tables or pair-share).

Main meeting: short presentations, like teachers helping teachers, kudos, or success stories, interspersed with small bits of talk from the principal or other figurehead talking; best thing to do is handle administrivia in a memo to be picked up on the way out the door; could have one "long" presentation (twenty minutes is a good maximum; perhaps focus on one department or a specific teaching strategy like jigsaw or reciprocal reading, which can be adapted to all content areas.

Do not have a sign-in or things to pick up on the way in; this takes too long. Assign someone trustworthy to take attendance (math teachers are especially good at this with their logical-mathematical skills). Have things on tables, ready to go, maybe even the food in small bowls.

Closure: exit slip, pair share, or one-word response to leader as you exit.

Follow-up: ask teachers to journal about this meeting and offer comments to facilitators (comments may be sent by e-mail); have facilitators visit each teacher informally one week after the inservice to have a five-minute follow-up discussion; send an e-mail two weeks later and ask everyone to respond with one thing you've done differently already as a result.

HALF-DAY INSERVICE OR LONG MEETING

Get ready ahead of time: coffee and breakfast foods or heavy snacks with soft, classical music playing; something pretty on each table, like a picture postcard, fresh flower, shell, or object connected to the day's objective; supplies or handouts on each table.

Warm-up: brain drain, morning pages, journal prompt or silent reading (of each person's own choice or material provided by leader); have a community circle when all arrive (this way everyone gets to know each other or refamiliarize themselves right from the start).

Main meeting: leader shares agenda or overview of the session; mixture of activities (at least two different ones, perhaps one loud and moving and one quiet and still).

Closure: exit slip or journal entry; read-aloud of affirming poem or other literature to send all participants off with good feelings.

Follow-up: same as for short meeting if inservice; if graduate course, some kind of homework for next class meeting, like reading in professional materials and/or writing a response.

FULL-DAY INSERVICE

Get ready ahead of time: food (breakfast and snack foods); go on the healthy side with some protein and some sugars.

Warm-up: same as short or long meetings above.

Make sure to provide several breaks. Breakfast on the way in, provided, but lunch away from the site. Very important. Teachers rarely get to do this, and it's a welcome treat. One morning break and one afternoon break. People get sleepy after a big lunch. Use the morning for quiet things, and the afternoon for more action and movement to combat sleepiness. Allow transition time when people straggle in from lunch. (Expect that one-third will be late.) This is a good time to have a reading assignment that will then be talked about with a jigsaw activity, story map, literature circle, etc.

Main meeting: leader shares agenda or overview of the session; mixture of activities (several different ones incorporating various intelligences, communication styles, and Myers-Briggs preferences).

Closure: always close on time at the latest, but strive to end ten minutes early; provide an evaluation form or have participants do a form of short, reflective writing.

Follow-up: the topic must be referred to in faculty meetings, department meetings, observations, etc. in order to take hold. Teachers resent having a daylong inservice and then never addressing the topic again. Make sure follow-up is planned and is consistent.

MULTIPLE-DAY INSERVICE OR GRADUATE CLASS

Get ready ahead of time: sense of ritual; beautiful objects and music and things that will provide ownership—plan ownership-type activities from day one; food, maybe with a potluck sign-up process (builds community to have shared, potluck meals and keeps the group together at lunch time); maybe have one or two special days with lunch at a nice local restaurant (these can be used in conjunction with celebrating some kind of success or completion of a major task).

Warm-up: should be similar every day or the same every day, as in, "We all come in and write for thirty minutes first thing every class period" (this builds a sense of continuity and predictability; can be comfortable).

Main meeting: variety of activities including presentations by teachers, individually and in groups.

Closure: ritual every day, like an exit slip or graffiti board.

Follow-up: e-mail distribution list or online bulletin board; coaches checking on participants at least once every few weeks.

Journal Prompts Used Successfully

From the Horry County Schools Curriculum Standards Pilot Project, 1994–1995

Your journal is a vital research and reflection tool. Please use the following questions as guidelines for writing in your journal.

A. How do you teach to the standards in your classroom? Describe particular lessons, resources, strategies, or plans you'd like to enact in the future and relate them to specific standards.
B. How do you apply multiple intelligences research in your classroom? Which of the intelligences do you feel you address well? Which are hard for you to address?
C. How do you utilize real-world and unpredictable experiences to make the work you assign relevant for your students?
D. Are there students you feel have mastered certain standards? Describe them and their work. Are there students you feel will have trouble meeting certain standards? Describe them and their work. Propose solutions.
E. What has been a successful lesson, project, unit, or activity in your classroom? Describe it and tell why you feel it was successful.

Nagging questions: How do we assess vocabulary in a more authentic, performance manner? How do we facilitate students having meaningful conferences about the content of their writing before they peer-edit? How do we manage to give all students adequate, meaningful time on the computers without turning the classroom into total chaos?

Working in a small group, develop a performance assessment you would like to implement. Write a description, including student hand-outs, rubrics, etc., and bring the draft next week for feedback.

Homework: Examine the "chunk" of learning you and your students are involved in right now. How will you assess their learning at the end of this "chunk"? Have you identified and communicated the expected learning? Respond in your journal.

Homework: Compare the state's standards to the county's draft. Where do we go from here? What are your recommendations? What are you considering for the model assessment you will soon write? How are you expanding your use of technology personally and with your students?

PROMPTS USED WITH VARIOUS GROUPS, 1998–2003

1. Identify a curricular "itch"—something you want to do differently in your classroom. Think about how you can research, write about, and talk about this "itch." It will be the basis for your professional piece and your presentation in this class.
2. Think about yourself as a learner. What conditions are necessary for you to learn best? For example, do you need clear directions, or do you prefer more open-ended tasks? Do you like to work alone or in groups—or a little bit of both? Do you prefer background noise or absolute quiet? How do you remember important things? How do you like to be assessed on what you have learned? After writing about your own learning, think about students who seem to learn like you do. Then think about students who seem to learn in different ways—or some who seem not to learn at all! Write about the different learners in your classroom. How can you apply what you know about your own learning to the young adults you teach? What lessons can be learned?
3. Think about these questions: How much time do I provide for talking and sharing among students (for example, community circle, peer response to drafts, etc.)? Can I realistically provide more? How? What will I need to give up?
4. What kinds of real-life, being-there experiences could I provide for my students, even if I can't take them away from campus?

5. How do I use reflective writing (exit slips, learning logs, etc.) in my classroom? How could I more often find out what students are thinking about their own learning?

6. How could I "celebrate" writing in my classroom? Reading? Learning in general?

7. How do I use the various modes of thinking/learning (writing, speaking, drawing, acting, etc.)? Do I rely only on certain ones, and if so, how could I incorporate others?

8. Think about this quote from Rainer Maria Rilke in *Letters to a Young Poet*: "Have patience with everything unresolved in your heart and try to love the questions themselves. . . . Live the questions now." How have you been "living the questions" in your classroom? What have you noticed? Have you had any "a-ha!" moments? How is your teaching metaphor evident? Is it changing?

9. "Shadow" another teacher for part of a day. (This requires your principal's help in covering your classes.) Write in your journal about this experience.

10. You've been reading a professional book. Describe how your professional reading has influenced your teaching. What are some of the powerful ideas you have encountered? How have you used them? Has your reading led you to any new discoveries? Has it led you to other professional resources?

11. Leave your journal somewhere in your classroom, open to a clean page each day. As you notice something that seems related to your inquiry question, jot yourself a quick note. At the end of the day, at lunchtime, or at the beginning of your planning period, take five minutes to write extended notes. Periodically look back on these notes and reflect upon them. Write more in-depth about things that seem particularly striking.

See appendix D for more journal prompt suggestions.

Teacher Inquiry Projects
Chabad Academy Faculty, 1998–1999

Teacher #1

Questions:

1. How do audiobooks help weak readers?
2. How can I encourage weak readers to enjoy reading more and to choose books they like to read?

Possible sources of data:

1. Observations of students engaged in listening to audiobooks, written responses to what they have read/listened to (journal entries, etc.), tests/quizzes
2. Observations of students

TEACHER #2

Questions:

1. How can I build a sense of community in my classes?
2. How can I use creative writing in Hebrew?
3. How can I use read-alouds in my classes?

Possible sources of data:

1. Observations of students, peer observations of the teacher, number of discipline problems tracked, informal discussion with students

2. Responses to assignments given in class
3. Observations of students

TEACHER #3

Questions:

1. How can I address the needs of accelerated learners while also meeting the needs of the rest of the class?
2. How can I use creative writing in Hebrew?

Possible sources of data:

1. Observations of accelerated students, informal discussions with accelerated students, examples of differentiated assignments and student work
2. Responses to assignments given in class

TEACHER #4

Question: How can I get my seventh/eighth grade students more engaged in their own learning?

Possible sources of data: Observations of students, surveys regarding their interests

TEACHER #5

Question: How can I get my students to edit their own work more effectively?

Possible sources of data: Various drafts of writing assignments, observations of students in the editing process, observations of students having peer editing conferences, notes on their editing conferences with the teacher, peer observations of the teacher having conferences and/or teaching editing mini-lessons

Beginning Inquiry at Your School

From a Presentation for Horry County Schools, November 2001

If you would like to encourage reflection about teaching and learning within your organization, I suggest some of the following methods that have been used with groups with whom I have worked.

Make time to talk with other teachers about your teaching. Remember to focus on the *students'* learning and *your* teaching; don't have "gripe sessions" that don't explore ways to improve practice. Seek out teachers whom you think have ideas you'd like to hear more about.

Use the Coalition of Essential Schools IITIC tools/protocols for discussions and writings with your colleagues. (Go to http://www.essentialschools.org/ and search using "IITIC" as your search term.)

Read the book *Mind Matters: Teaching for Thinking* by Kirby and Kuykendall, and do some of the activities yourself or with colleagues.

Videotape your own teaching and watch the video. What do you see? How is it different from what you expected to see? What changes would you like to make?

Read something with the whole faculty, one department, a small group of colleagues, or even just one colleague or teaching friend and discuss it, focusing on the student learning. Resources I've used include articles from *Educational Leadership, Phi Delta Kappan, English Journal,* and various state and national standards documents (including *The South Carolina Frameworks for the English Language Arts*).

Allow, encourage, or even require that teachers in your organization observe each other teach at least twice during the school year. Support this initiative with time, substitutes to cover classes, and meaningful follow-up conversation.

At faculty meetings, during staff development days, at faculty retreats, etc., make time for writing and/or conversation based on prompts like the following:

1. Who was the best teacher you ever had? The worst? How did they influence your *learning?* How did they influence your *teaching?*
2. Think/write/talk about the best lesson you taught recently. Why was it so good? What did you learn about your students' *learning?* What did you learn about your own *teaching?*
3. Discuss one of your most memorable students, either good or bad. Why does this person stick with you? What did you learn from him/her?
4. Discuss a professional role model. What admirable qualities does this person have? How are you like/unlike this person?

Examples of Book Discussion Meeting Agendas

CHABAD ACADEMY, 17 OCTOBER 2001

Book Discussion of *Classroom Instruction That Works*

Chapter 1

Central premise: Effective teachers make a difference in student achievement, regardless of other factors (socioeconomic status, family situations, race/ethnicity, prior learning, etc.).

Let's discuss: What is your reaction to this central premise?

Nine proven effective strategies:

- identifying similarities and differences
- summarizing/note-taking
- providing reinforcement/recognition
- assigning practice
- using visual representations
- using cooperative learning
- providing feedback
- testing hypotheses
- cues and advance organizers

Chapter 2

Let's discuss: How have you helped your students identify similarities and differences recently?

Identifying similarities and differences may be done in four main ways:

Comparison: teacher-directed or student-directed; Venn diagrams and matrices.

Classification: teacher-directed or student-directed; charts.

Metaphor: teacher-directed or student-directed; writing and visual symbols (for example, the "hamburger" model of a paragraph).

Analogy: teacher-directed or student-directed; graphic organizers.

Ideas:

1. Be conscious of times when you are teaching (or should teach) about similarities and differences.
2. Use a visual/graphic organizer the next time you discuss similarities and differences with your students.
3. Record what happens in your teaching journal and discuss it at the next faculty meeting.

CHABAD ACADEMY, 14 NOVEMBER 2001

Book Discussion: *Classroom Instruction That Works*

We'll write in our teaching journals until everyone arrives.

Writing Prompt: Think about yourself as a learner. When you have to remember something important, how do you do study and take notes? Do the ways you personally learn apply to the learning of your students? How?

(Real-life example: My husband and I recently remodeled a bathroom. In order to make a decision on a whirlpool tub, I read many brochures and booklets. I did research online. We made comparison charts and took other notes. These notes helped us make decisions about what features we wanted, what brand of tub to buy, etc. In my journal, I will write about how my real-life learning could apply to my teaching as I help students make comparisons, analyze, and evaluate.)

Chapter 3: Summarizing and Note Taking

Central premise: We must help students learn to summarize and take notes effectively because these skills are important in all subject areas and outside school as well.

Key points: Students must learn to delete extraneous information in order to summarize. Students must analyze information in order to summarize. Students must learn that information is presented in an explicit form or structure. Verbatim notetaking is ineffective. Notes can and should be revised. Notes should be used to study for tests.

Effective strategies:

- Rule-based summary strategy
- Frames (p. 35–41)
- Reciprocal teaching
- Teacher-prepared notes
- Outlines
- Webs
- Combination notes
- *Mind-mapping (see supplemental handout)
- *Somebody Wanted But So (see supplemental handout)
- *Not discussed in the book

Mind Mapping (Information adapted from *How to Think Like Leonardo da Vinci: Seven Steps to Genius Every Day* by Michael Gelb):

1. Begin with a blank page. Using it horizontally gives you more room.
2. Make sure you have access to different colors of pens, pencils, or markers.
3. In the center, draw an image to represent your subject. Draw it as vividly as possible.
4. Print key words or draw images on lines radiating from the center. If you use words, use only one key word at a time. Break everything down to its simplest, most easily remembered visual form.
5. Draw branches from your key words as ideas come to you. Again, use key words and/or images on the branches. A mind map is meant to be primarily visual and should not be overcrowded with words. Don't worry about being "right." Just keep the ideas flowing.

6. Keep going until you run out of ideas.
7. Examine your map. Eliminate ideas that seem extraneous. Find words or images that repeat. These may suggest major themes.
8. Connect related parts of your map by color, arrows, numbers, or another scheme you come up with.
9. Study your mind map as needed to prepare for tests, remember key ideas, etc.

CHABAD ACADEMY, 13 MARCH 2002

Quiet journal writing time:

1. Do a "brain drain" to write away the day's stresses and concerns if you need to, or respond to this prompt: What is one thing entirely within your control that you could do to improve your school?
2. We'll discuss your journal writing at the end of our meeting.

Classroom Instruction That Works by Robert Marzano, et al.

1. Discussion of chapter 6, "Nonlinguistic Representations." Knowledge is stored in two forms: linguistic and imagery. Nonlinguistic forms include graphic representations, physical models, mental pictures, drawn pictures/visuals, kinesthetic activities, etc.
2. Share successful nonlinguistic activities that you've used (see below for my example).

Nonlinguistic Representation Example: Story Portrait

1. Work alone or with a partner reading the same book.
2. Draw a border to frame your portrait. Use symbols, colors, or key words that reveal something about the book.
3. Draw a symbol of something important in the center of your story portrait. This should relate to plot, characterization, or theme.
4. Write a significant quotation from the book somewhere in the portrait.

5. Put the book title somewhere in the portrait.
6. Add other pictures or symbols as needed to represent the theme of the book.
7. Present your story portrait in your assigned small group. Give a three to five minute presentation.

CHABAD ACADEMY, 24 APRIL 2002

Book Discussion: *Learning by Heart* by Roland Barth

Chapter 2: Culture in Question

1. "Nondiscussables," (p. 9). Do you have "nondiscussables" at your school? What are some of them, and how could we better deal with them? What does the phrase "community of learners" (p. 12) mean to you?
2. "Learn or we will hurt you," (p.16). In what ways is this message passed along? Are you a true lifelong learner?

Chapter 3: A Community of Learners

1. The role of parents (p. 24).
2. "You can't lead where you won't go," (p. 27). What does this mean to you? How does it apply to teaching?
3. Being a "leading learner," (p. 28). Do you do this? How?

Chapter 4: Information Rich and Experience Poor

1. Transmission of Knowledge model (p. 31).
2. Activity and joy in learning (p. 35).
3. Eighty-five percent of the talk in classrooms is teacher talk. What are the implications of this?

Chapter 5: Exploration

1. Boats and schools (p. 42).
2. MET School (p. 44).
3. Experiential model (p. 48).

Chapter 6: Craft Knowledge

1. Legitimate learning (p. 54).
2. Breadth vs. depth (p. 55).

Chapter 7: Reflection

1. "To reflect on practice we must observe practice," (p. 66).
2. Using writing to reflect (p. 67).

Example of Transcript of an Excellent Teacher

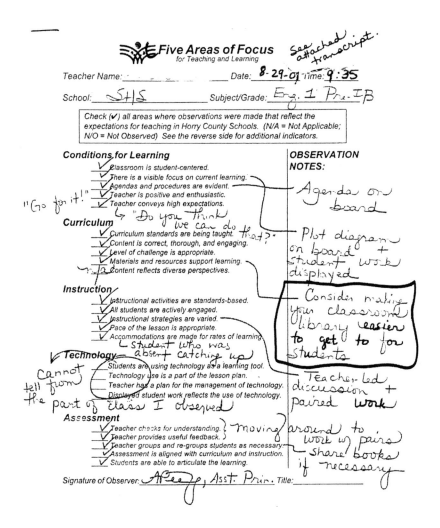

See attached transcript.

Five Areas of Focus
for Teaching and Learning

Teacher Name: _____ Date: 8-29-01 Time: 9:35

School: SHS Subject/Grade: Eng. 1 Pre-IB

Check (✔) all areas where observations were made that reflect the expectations for teaching in Horry County Schools. (N/A = Not Applicable; N/O = Not Observed) See the reverse side for additional indicators.

Conditions for Learning
- ✔ Classroom is student-centered.
- ✔ There is a visible focus on current learning.
- ✔ Agendas and procedures are evident.
- ✔ Teacher is positive and enthusiastic.
- ✔ Teacher conveys high expectations.

"Go for it!"

↳ "Do you think we can do that?"

Curriculum
- ✔ Curriculum standards are being taught.
- ✔ Content is correct, thorough, and engaging.
- ✔ Level of challenge is appropriate.
- ✔ Materials and resources support learning.
- n/a Content reflects diverse perspectives.

Instruction
- ✔ Instructional activities are standards-based.
- ✔ All students are actively engaged.
- ✔ Instructional strategies are varied.
- ✔ Pace of the lesson is appropriate.
- ✔ Accommodations are made for rates of learning.

Student who was absent catching up

Technology
- Students are using technology as a learning tool.
- Technology use is a part of the lesson plan.
- Teacher has a plan for the management of technology.
- Displayed student work reflects the use of technology.

Cannot tell from the part of class I observed

Assessment
- ✔ Teacher checks for understanding.
- ✔ Teacher provides useful feedback.
- ✔ Teacher groups and re-groups students as necessary.
- ✔ Assessment is aligned with curriculum and instruction.
- ✔ Students are able to articulate the learning.

Signature of Observer: _____, Asst. Prin. Title: _____

OBSERVATION NOTES:

Agenda on board

Plot diagram on board + student work displayed

Consider making your classroom library easier to get to for students

Teacher-led discussion + paired work

moving around to work in pairs - share books if necessary

8-29

9:35 Discussing fear) w/ students
"So, it's about winning +
losing? ... Is there a
deeper message here? ...
philosophical ... what do I
mean by that word?"
"The boat became) your
metaphor... that is your
philosophy..."
Student
"... The literature should speak to
you about life..."
2) students
Will do read-aloud — students will stop
him when philosophy is evident
9:40 Teacher starts reading)
9:42 Students say "stop".
"Do you see how it shifts there?"
"In groups of 2, go through the story
again... jot it down... helps us
understand the characters...";
Brings student in (or checks on) student in
hallway
9:47 Students are paired up + working)   "Stop...
Teacher circulating)   we'll start
                                          w/ this
"Right — that's a belief system..."   activity
"I found another one... go back to p.14... tomorrow..."
Chock full... see if you can find it..."

Using Transcription to Document Incompetence

This teacher was in the process of being denied a contract when she chose to retire. Here is an outline of the two-year process of dismissal.

1. Along with a district-level supervisor, I observed one of her classes early in the year for about ten minutes.
2. As suggested by the district-level supervisor, I sent a memo and my notes about the observation to the teacher and met with her as follow-up.
3. A district-level subject area coordinator began to observe in the classes at least once a month as well.
4. I did a twenty-minute observation a few weeks after the observation listed in step number one and transcribed what was happening. I provided these notes to the teacher and asked two other assistant principals to make drop-in visits of ten to fifteen minutes to see if they had similar concerns. I met with the teacher again and made specific suggestions for improvement.
5. I wrote a formal memo to the principal, requesting that the teacher meet with both him and me to discuss my concerns.
6. The three of us met, and the principal expressed his hope that things would improve or he would have to place her on formal evaluation the following year.
7. I did at least one more twenty-minute observation and provided the transcription to the teacher. Other administrators continued to drop in and monitor the classes regularly.
8. The teacher was placed on formal evaluation.
9. The teacher was assigned a three-person evaluation team,

including me, which observed her repeatedly during the first semester. In the meeting before Christmas holidays, we found her unsatisfactory in several areas and assigned specific professional growth tasks for her to complete, including videotaping a class period, watching it privately, responding to it in writing, and then meeting with the two administrators on her evaluation team.

10. The teacher repeatedly avoided taping the class, so I enlisted the assistance of a media specialist and had a different class videotaped. I asked the teacher to watch the video, respond to it in writing, and then meet with me and the other administrator on her team.

11. The teacher did not meet with me or the other administrator but did provide a written response to the tape, which did not address the many problems evident in the class (students off task, students sleeping, students having conversations with their friends during direct instruction, the teacher violating school rules regarding hall passes, etc.).

12. The evaluation team continued to observe and to transcribe notes as part of the documentation process.

13. In April, the teacher was found unsatisfactory again and was told by the evaluation team that she would have to meet with the principal regarding her contract status.

14. The principal initiated actions to deny the teacher a contract for the following year.

Here is the text of the original memo of concern I sent (step number two above):

Attached are notes I took as Mr. _____ and I visited your classroom Monday. I would like to meet with you at your convenience to discuss the observation.

Specifically, when we meet, let's discuss the following: the use of a daily agenda, the seating arrangement, and student involvement in the learning activities.

I'm available to meet during your planning period Friday or Monday. I look forward to talking with you.

Here are the notes I attached to that memo:

We enter the classroom at 11:13. The teacher is discussing *Huckleberry Finn* with the students. She is reading from papers she holds in her hand.

The room is arranged with a square within a square. The teacher sits in the inside square with her back to three students who sit with their backs to the chalkboard. There is one row of desks over by the computers. Four students are sitting in these desks.

One student, Holly, is asleep.

There is a list of thirty root words on the board. I do not see a daily agenda posted. Some of the first-period teacher's handwriting is on the board as well.

11:16—The teacher stands and continues to read from the papers in her hand. Some students (about half the class) have their textbooks open. Some students are looking at a handout. Student work is displayed on the back wall of the classroom. The boy seated beside me is reading a short story in his textbook.

The teacher says, "The next ones, we can start working on them now. . . . The page numbers may or may not correspond to the edition you have . . . I'm not sure. Start reading today. . . . Some of you I'm going to send to the library because you didn't bring a book. . . . Answer the questions for chapters 1–10 by the day after tomorrow. . . . Hang on to the handouts. Don't lose these. . . ."

We left the classroom at 11:23. Holly woke up right before we left, got a hall pass from the teacher, and left the room.

The following illustrations show the district observation form I used in January along with my transcription and memo to the principal (step numbers four and five above).

Observation of ██████████

I entered class a̶ 9:17 This is an English 2 yearlong class. As I entered, a boy in the back row took off his hat and smiled at me as I whispered "thank you" to him for removing it.   **not following school rules**

The teacher was calling out questions; students were writing them down. The teacher spelled out the words "scar" and "plea" when she used them. She also wrote two of the characters' names on the board so they could see the correct spelling. The teacher was reading the questions from a sheet that looked like it came from a teacher materials packet or workbook of some kind. (Suggestion: to save time, have the questions prepared on an overhead transparency, handout, or on the board ahead of time.)

One boy in back corner, 1st row, was not doing anything but staring into space--others were writing the questions on notebook paper.

I noticed that the three black students in the class all sit together in the back corner and wondered if the class has assigned or self-chosen seats.

Students called out their book numbers and the teacher recorded them in her gradebook. Not all students had books. M████ and the girl across from her passed a Mello Yello back and forth and then the girl (not M████) brushed her hair.

"N████, start us out please on p. 7..." J██ volunteered and read instead for 2-3 mins. The teacher told the boy in the corner to sit beside another boy and handed them a book to use. The teacher began to read aloud to the class.

9:30
Teacher tapped one boy on his head (which was down on the desk) and whistled at him; he sat up and started following along in his book again. To two others (J███ and the boy beside him) she said, "You gettin' this by osmosis?" as they laid their heads down. They picked their heads up but J███ laid his back down shortly afterwards--his book was open and he appeared to be following along, not sleeping.

9:35
Teacher was still reading aloud and dramatizing. Most students were paying close attention, and some were laughing as she dramatized the characters' voices.

There were 30 vocab. words on the board but no daily agenda posted. Written on the board: "Psychology: Observation due Fri. Chap. 1 due Thurs. Be prepared to discuss major theories."

I left the class a̶ 9:38

20 mins.

* Transcript attached

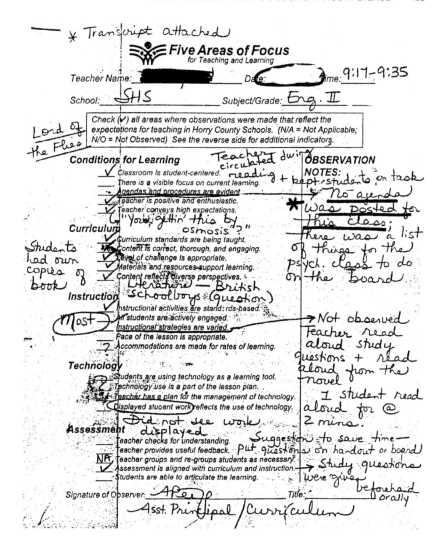

Five Areas of Focus
for Teaching and Learning

Teacher Name: ▓▓▓▓▓ Date: ⬯ Time: 9:17–9:35

School: SHS   Subject/Grade: Eng. II

Lord of the Flies

Check (✔) all areas where observations were made that reflect the expectations for teaching in Horry County Schools. (N/A = Not Applicable; N/O = Not Observed) See the reverse side for additional indicators.

Conditions for Learning   *Teacher circulated dwi reading + kept students on task*   **OBSERVATION NOTES:**

✔ Classroom is student-centered.
__ There is a visible focus on current learning.
•_ Agendas and procedures are evident.   *No agenda was posted for this class; there was a list of things for the psych. class to do on the board*
✔ Teacher is positive and enthusiastic.
✔ Teacher conveys high expectations.

"You're gettin' this by osmosis?"

Curriculum

_ Curriculum standards are being taught.
__ Content is correct, thorough, and engaging.
✔ Level of challenge is appropriate.
✔ Materials and resources support learning.
✔ Content reflects diverse perspectives.

Students had own copies of book

Literature — British schoolboys (question)

Instruction

✔ Instructional activities are standards-based.
_ All students are actively engaged.
_ Instructional strategies are varied.   → *Not observed*
_ Pace of the lesson is appropriate.   *Teacher read aloud study questions + read aloud from the novel*
? Accommodations are made for rates of learning.

Most

Technology

_ Students are using technology as a learning tool.   *1 student read aloud for @ 2 mins.*
_ Technology use is a part of the lesson plan.
_ Teacher has a plan for the management of technology.
_ Displayed student work reflects the use of technology.   *Suggestion - to save time — Put questions on handout or board*

Did not see work displayed

Assessment

_ Teacher checks for understanding.
_ Teacher provides useful feedback.   → *Study questions were given beforehand orally*
NA Teacher groups and re-groups students as necessary.
✔ Assessment is aligned with curriculum and instruction.
_ Students are able to articulate the learning.

Signature of Observer: A Pe__   Title: Asst. Principal / Curriculum

To: Paul Browning

From: Angela Peery

Re: Concerns

I would like to share some concerns about Mrs. ████████classes in the hopes that we may all work together to improve the situation.

Specifically, I am concerned about the following.
- A general lack of awareness about people's whereabouts (both students and administrators enter and leave the room without being acknowledged by the teacher)
- The level of student engagement (students sleeping and being off-task)
- The English 2 students' EOC scores and evidence folders
- A high failure rate first semester
- Mrs. ██████ failure to follow school procedures (for hall passes, guidance referrals, and administrative referrals)

My concerns are based mainly on drop-in observations of Aug. 24, Dec. 4, and Jan. 11 plus my meeting with ██████████ and ██████████ on Feb. 8.

Inservice Strategies

COMMUNITY CIRCLE

This strategy is described fully in the book *Tribes: A New Way of Learning Together* by Jeanne Gibbs. Community circle is a way to build inclusion and teach social skills. It may be used with any age level and in any subject area. The agreements for community circle time are the following: Listen attentively. Show appreciation (don't use put-downs). You always have the right to pass. Show mutual respect.

To begin, all participants sit in a circle or other formation so that everyone sees each other. The facilitator asks a "question of the day" or sets the focus for the discussion. Everyone responds in turn. Those who pass on the first time around are invited to respond after everyone else has responded. The leader facilitates the discussion but does not repeat, paraphrase, or comment on anyone's contributions until everyone has shared. Circle members may ask questions of and express appreciation to individuals at the end of the sharing.

Community circle is a good strategy to start or end a class or meeting. Generally, it can last as few as five minutes or as many as thirty. Active listening skills and public speaking skills are reinforced through frequent use of community circle with students.

Sample topics I've used successfully with both adults and teenagers:

1. Share some of your favorite and/or least favorite activities in past classes or inservices like this. (No individuals' names, please.)
2. What is one of your favorite books or stories—even from childhood?

3. Share something unique about you.
4. Share something you are proud of or good at doing.
5. What is something you're looking forward to this year in school?
6. What is something you want to learn in this class?
7. Share something interesting from your reading today (a significant quote, a surprising event, etc.).
8. Name something you learned in class today.
9. One goal I have for my future is . . .
10. Read aloud or tell about something in your journal.
11. Discuss a recent school event (guest speaker, assembly, etc.).
12. My favorite (topic to teach, author, food, song, TV show, character in a book, poet, etc.) is _____ because . . .
13. What questions will you leave this class or inservice with today?

ENTRANCE AND EXIT SLIPS

Entrance slips are written at the beginning of an inservice in response to a prompt posed by the leader. Exit slips are written at the end and may serve as "tickets" out the door. Here are actual examples from my work.

Faculty Meeting, Fall 2002

The following was on the overhead and people responded by writing on index cards at their seats. Their responses and my discussion of their responses opened the meeting.

Entrance Slip: On your index card, write two sentences about writing instruction in your classroom. Sign your name only if you want to. We'll discuss your answers in a few minutes. Examples:

. (declarative)	I ask my students to write meaningfully every day.
. (imperative)	Show me how to teach this writing stuff.
! (exclamatory)	Geez, more talk about writing! Get over it, already!
? (interrogative)	Lady, what more do you want me to do?

PEOPLE HUNT

This is a scavenger hunt-type activity that gets people moving. Have the questions on a handout and provide one handout for each participant.

People Hunt

Travel around the room and find people who fit the following descriptions. Have each person sign his or her name in the space provided. Use at least five *different* people to answer these questions. Find someone who . . .

1. Does not watch much TV.
2. Is very artistic.
3. Can touch his/her nose with his/her tongue.
4. Has more than three pets.
5. Has a birthday within two months of yours.
6. Has a young child in his/her household.
7. Was not born in this state.
8. Was born in this state.
9. Lives in a home where no one smokes.
10. Has a part-time job.

FOUR CORNERS

You need to have 4×6 or 5×8 index cards or paper cut to a similar size for this activity. Have participants answer four questions, putting one answer in each corner of the card or paper. In the middle of the rectangle, each person puts his or her first name, very large so others can see. After sharing, have everyone wear their cards like nametags, display them on the table (standing up), or tape to the front of the desk. This is a great way to learn names fast. Sample questions:

1. What is your favorite food (book, class to teach, etc.)?
2. What is the last movie you saw?
3. What is a special talent you have?

4. What is one of your favorite hobbies or leisure activities?
5. What is something you're proud of?
6. What is something you are looking forward to this year?

QUICK WRITES

A quick write is just that: you start writing, based on whatever prompt or directions the presenter gave you, and you try to write nonstop until time is called.

You may ask for volunteers to discuss what they wrote about after a quick write; however, encourage them *not* to read their writing aloud. Because the writing happens so quickly, most people are uncomfortable reading it word for word.

References

Armstrong, Thomas. 1996. *Multiple Intelligences in the Classroom.* Alexandria, Va.: ASCD.

———. 1999. *Seven Kinds of Smart: Identifying and Developing Your Multiple Intelligences.* New York: Plume.

Checkley, K. 1997. "The First Seven . . . and an Eighth: A Conversation with Howard Gardner." *Educational Leadership* 55, no. 1, http://www.ascd.org/readingroom/edlead/9709/checkley.html (accessed 30 September 2003).

Coalition of Essential Schools National Web. Improving Instruction through Inquiry and Collaboration, http://ces.edgateway.net/cs/resources/view/ces_res/264 (accessed 24 September 2003).

Darling-Hammond, Linda. "Teacher Learning That Supports Student Learning." *Educational Leadership,* http://www.ascd.org/readingroom/edlead/9802/toc.html (accessed 30 September 2003).

———. "Teacher Quality and Student Achievement: A Review of State Policy Evidence." *Education Policy Analysis Archives* 8, no. 1, http://epaa.asu.edu/epaa/v8n1/ (accessed 30 September 2003).

Fullan, Michael. 1993. *Change Forces: Probing the Depths of Educational Reform.* Bristol, Pa.: Falmer Press.

Fullan, Michael, with Suzanne Stiegelbauer. 1991. *The New Meaning of Educational Change.* New York: Teachers College Press.

Gardner, Howard. 1993. *Frames of Mind: The Theory of Multiple Intelligences.* New York: Basic Books.

Gibbs, Jeanne. 1994. *Tribes: A New Way of Learning Together.* Santa Rosa, Calif.: Center Source Publishing.

Kirby, Dan, and Kuykendall, Cathy. 1991. *Mind Matters: Teaching for Thinking.* Portsmouth, N.H.: Boynton/Cook.

Knowles, M. 1984. *The Adult Learner: A Neglected Species.* 3rd ed. Houston, Tex.: Gulf Publishing.

Lieberman, Ann. 2000. "Teachers Transforming Teaching: Stories, Strategies, and Structures." Speech delivered at the Teaching for Thinking Conference, Orlando, Fla.

———. 2002. "Teachers as Learners and Leaders: Professional Development That Matters." Speech delivered at the University of Las Vegas, http://www.nevadarea.org/lieberman.html (accessed 30 September 2003).

National Staff Development Council. 2001. Standards for staff development, http://www.nsdc.org/educatorindex.htm (accessed 30 September 2003).

Palmer, Parker. 1997. "The Heart of a Teacher." *Change Magazine* 29, no. 6 (November/December): 14–21. Reprint, Washington, D. C.: Heldref.

———. 1999. "Good Talk about Good Teaching." http://www.teacher-formation.org/html/rr/intro-f.cfm (accessed 30 September 2003).

———. 2000. *Let Your Life Speak: Listening for the Voice of Vocation.* San Francisco: Jossey-Bass.

Peery, Angela. 2000. *Redefining Professional Development as Teacher Inquiry: The Chabad Academy's Approach.* Unpublished doctoral dissertation, University of South Carolina.

Schlechty, Phil. 1993. "On the Frontier of School Reform with Trailblazers, Pioneers, and Settlers." *Journal of Staff Development* 14, no. 4: 46–51.

Schön, Donald. 1983. *The Reflective Practitioner: How Professionals Think in Action.* New York: Basic Books.

———. 1987. *Educating the Reflective Practitioner: Toward a New Design for Teaching and Learning in the Professions.* San Francisco: Jossey-Bass.

Index

About the Author

Angela Peery is a teacher specialist for the South Carolina Department of Education, adjunct faculty member of the Graduate School of Education at Coastal Carolina University, codirector of the Coastal Area Writing Project, and a former high school English teacher and assistant principal. When not engaged in teaching, research, or writing, she enjoys the natural beauty of South Carolina's Lowcountry with her husband and pets.